Book Marketing
Secrets

The 10 fundamental secrets for selling more books and creating a successful book publishing career

Claim Your Surprise Gift

Thank you so much for purchasing my book. To show my appreciation, I've prepared a special gift for you that will help you to sell more books. Access it by visiting: www.albertgriesmayr.com/thank-you

About The Author

Albert Griesmayr (MBA) is founder & CEO of the book publishing startup Scribando | Novelify. It has proudly helped more than 10,000 authors to create successful book projects since 2013. He personally has consulted for more than 100 authors, among them bestselling- and award-winning authors, such as BC Schiller, Patrick McKeown, and Garret Kramer, with combined sales of more than 2 million copies. His company Scribando | Novelify was selected as a 2013 participant of the Go Silicon Valley initiative of the Austrian Chamber of Commerce.

In addition, he is the innovative creator of the book marketing initiatives "Lean Book Publishing" and "Who-Wrote-It". He shares his latest book marketing insights on scribando.com and albertgriesmayr.com, and is a frequent speaker at global book marketing events.

X- Note From The Author

Hello author,

It's great getting to know you. First of all, I want to extend my gratitude to you for purchasing my book. This book contains my most valuable and timeless secrets for making your book successful. This is knowledge that I've proactively acquired by helping more than 10,000 authors to market their books successfully through my book publishing platforms over the last 10 years. It embodies lots of timeless knowledge, tactics and strategies that, applied correctly, would have made your book successful not only in 2019, but earlier as well. My goal is that it'll also make your book successful in 2020, 2025, and hopefully even in 2030 and later. I will certainly update the book over time, and make sure it stays on top to deliver you and your book the cutting edge you need to succeed in the changing book publishing landscape.

Before jumping right into the 10 book marketing secrets, I want to use this chance to quickly introduce myself and to share with you why this book is so important to me.

So who am I? My name is Albert Griesmayr, and I'm the founder of the book publishing startup Scribando | Novelify which focuses on helping writers to sell more books. Besides this, I'm the creator of Lean Book Publishing [leanbookpublishing.com], Who-Wrote-It [who-wrote-it.com], and the Modern IQ [modern-iq.com].

Over the last 10 years, I have been fortunate enough to work personally with more than a hundred authors and publishers from around the world. I have helped them to create winning book marketing strategies and shared my insights with them along their publishing journeys. Helping authors and working with them is immensely rewarding to me.

There is one thing, though, that keeps hurting me. And this is seeing authors with great book ideas and everything necessary to make it big, failing because they did not know about the fundamentals and underlying secrets behind successful book publishing before they embarked on their journey.

That's why I decided to write this book. With this book, I want to offer you as an author a comprehensive guide that helps you to master the fundamentals of successful book publishing and book marketing.

I hope this book will offer you immense value. The information here has certainly facilitated my role as a book marketing consultant. Not only do I know all these secrets by heart, but I also apply them in my daily practices while working with authors. I'm confident that if you follow the advice in this book, you'll not only sell more books, but also become a better author as well. Book marketing is unique, and yet fundamentally similar to any product marketing. That's why you will find insights in this book that apply to marketing other products as well, and which are beneficial for other areas of business. I wish you the best for your continuing career as an author! Make sure to take a look at scribando.com and albertgriesmayr.com, where I deliver the latest strategies about how to succeed in the quick-changing book publishing landscape. And don't hesitate to send me an email sharing your questions or feedback with me.

Best wishes,
Albert Griesmayr
Founder & CEO of Scribando | Novelify
Vienna, Austria, January 1, 2020

Contents

📖 Foreword

*I*t was 2008. A windy, chilly morning. I was tired, but felt fulfilled. I had made it. I had finished my novel, 180 pages of the story that I had always wanted to write, in only 3 months, but with full focus. I had spent long days and nights alone, working and writing more than 18 hours a day, often staying up until 4 in the morning. I had been completely immersed in my story for 90 days. Having finished the book felt like an enormous victory to me. And it was. It felt good. And more than 10 years later I realize that writing my novel was one of the most fulfilling experiences I have ever encountered.

To keep the story short: the book never became a major success. It maybe sold 300 copies, was featured in a student newspaper, and filled my mom with pride. But it did not become the major bestseller which first time authors normally dream about. Unfortunately.

However, I learned two important lessons that would prove priceless for the upcoming years to follow:

1) How wonderful the immense feeling of fulfillment which comes from writing your own story is.

2) How hard it is to market a book successfully without any prior experience.

It was the early days of self-publishing. Not only was it clear that marketing was changing rapidly, but even more that authors were looking for help to navigate the landscape.

What followed was that I decided to focus my business career on book publishing, with the goal of helping authors. I founded my startup, Scribando, to help authors to find more success launching their books. My company quickly found clients and was selected by the Austrian government in 2013 as a participating startup at Go Silicon Valley.

I also founded initiatives like Lean Book Publishing, which aimed to bring the Lean Startup Movement to books.

Going forward almost 8 years, the book publishing landscape has changed dramatically. Amazon has become a giant of book e-commerce and self-publishing has become a serious alternative, even for the most respected authors and business professionals.

Writers are a lot more educated when it comes to book marketing and understanding the business of book publishing. However, there is still a lot of space for helping authors to succeed.

What I do with Scribando is make sure that authors are up-to-date on the market. However, with this book, I want to cover the fundamentals. These fundamentals are often timeless and very critical for the success of a book. Basically, it comes down to understanding the secrets of product marketing and combining that knowledge with profound experience in book marketing.

These fundamentals are about acknowledging that book publishing is as much a business nowadays as it is about being an artist. Marketing and publishing go hand-in-hand and cannot be seen as isolated from each other. Great book marketing results are mostly the result of process thinking, applying lean practices, good planning from the start, and lots of persistence when it comes to marketing and improving books over the years after launch.

Writers, if you have just launched your book, that was just the beginning.

I am happy to be able to accompany you on your journey. I hope this book is of as much value to you as it is to me in my daily practice of helping authors from around the world sell more books and achieve more success with their book projects.

1

⌞☆ The Book Is The Star

*B*ook Marketing Secret #1 is to understand that the book is the star. Always and always. It always comes down to the book. It is the groundwork that you lay for everything to come. Keep Secret #1 in mind at all times and you will be rewarded. Create a fantastic book that you are proud of. Your readers will thank you and reward you. True perennial bestsellers are great books. There is no exception to the rule.

But let's take a closer look at what "the book is the star" means. First of all, it means that the product you are selling is the book that you have. If I take your book away, you will have nothing to sell. You will stand naked. Understanding this automatically shifts your focus towards your book, which is the second important aspect. "The book is the star" also refers to a mindset of focusing on your book, instead of activities around it, like advertising campaigns, PR, book funnels, readings, etc.

From my experience working personally with more than a hundred authors from around the world, most books fall short when I see them the first time for a consulting session. And it's not because I expect too much! Most of the time, the authors I talk to are also not entirely convinced about the books they have created. After the initial call, on average only 1 out of 5 books need just a little polishing. Most books undergo deeper optimization, such as a new cover and improved first 10 pages. And improving the book is the best thing an author and publisher can do for success.

Your book is the most powerful weapon you have for making your book successful. It sounds obvious, but just visit Amazon.com and open some random niche and you will see what I mean. Publishers and authors still make too many shortcuts in this respect.

But I am not here to blame. We all have busy lives and many priorities. Just the ability to finish a book is a big victory that many people who want to never achieve. It's logical to try to get books on the market, so when the writer feels they are good enough, they move forward. But the point I want to make is that true book publishing experts know that every shortcut you make with your book will hurt you later.

When doing paid advertising, you will have to pay a higher CPC, your reviews will have lower ratings, you might have to correct issues with typos or the layout, try harder to convince a journalist to cover your story, and the list goes on and on. Too often, book projects fail because the initial launch does not bring the satisfaction an author wants. He moves on, leaving behind a book which has far more potential, but which never got the attention it would need to truly shine. Or, on the other hand, a neglected book needs a costly makeover and re-launch years later in order to fix what was an obvious problem right from the beginning, just because it wasn't taken seriously enough.

So in my role as a book marketing consultant, whenever a client comes to me, the book is the first thing I look at. I look at the 7 book marketing keys, which you will discover in Chapter 2, and the manuscript itself. That's where my work begins. I help the publisher or author to improve the book so that it shines. Because that profoundly affects everything that follows.

One of my favorite sayings in coaching calls is, "Every dollar spent in the book is worth more than the same dollar spent in advertising." And this is true in almost all cases.

"Every dollar spent in the book is worth more than the same dollar spent in advertising."

So if the quality of the book is so important, the question arises whether it is at all possible to become successful with an average or even a bad book. Well, the honest answer is yes. At least, in the short run it is possible. However, it requires a good advertising budget, an experienced publishing house, a celebrity endorsement, or book marketing pros to achieve success with mediocre books.

And what's more: a good book will always pay off more. Because it will create word-of-mouth, positive reviews, lower CPCs, and happier stakeholders on all sides. The best long-term investment in your publishing career you can make today is to tackle any known issues with your book and to make your book fantastic.

To further illustrate the power of a great book, I want to give insights into two popular books you're probably familiar with, which only found their way to success because of their true inner strength.

The first book I want to talk about is J.K. Rowling's *Harry Potter*, the best-selling book series in history. At this time of writing (October 30, 2019), it has sold more than 500 million copies worldwide.

You might think that the success is due to the fact that there's no way a book like that could possibly be overlooked by experienced publishing houses. But that couldn't be further from the truth.

Did you know that the book was turned down by 12 publishers before being accepted?[1] That J.K. Rowling received rejection notes advising her to take a writing course? That even the small British publisher Bloomsbury which eventually accepted *Harry Potter* was skeptical of its commercial potential in the beginning?

It was not until the chairman of the publishing house gave the first chapter to his then eight-year-old daughter, who then demanded to read more and more, that the book was accepted and the commercial potential seen.

Once *Harry Potter* was in the hands of its target audience, everything changed and the rest is history.

---

[1] Source: https://riseupeight.org/jk-rowling-harry-potter-books/

Harry Potter is a great example of "the book is the star". Not only does it show that a great story can quickly find acceptance once in the hands of its true target audience, but it also demonstrates how great writing can turn a new book, by an unknown author, into a bestseller in just a few weeks, largely by word of mouth.

The second book I want to talk about is *Chicken Soup For The Soul* by Jack Canfield, an inspirational book that contains 101 heartwarming stories. I still remember the recommendation which came from a close friend, not normally the kind of guy to read this kind of book. So I bought it myself, read it in a couple of days, and was impressed. It really is a beautiful and inspiring book. The commercial success it had proved that. What's interesting about the book, though, is not just that 144 publishers turned down the book initially. Even more intriguing is that what drove initial interest was not media attention or celebrity endorsement, but word-of-mouth from people who bought the book and loved it.

In just a few months *Chicken Soup For The Soul* sold so many copies that it appeared on almost all major bestseller lists in the USA and Canada. Today more than 500 million copies have been sold of the first title alone[2].

Chicken Soup For The Soul is a fantastic book, because people love the stories and it really touched the pulse of the time it was published. It was just a perfect match. It filled a niche gap and had a team behind it who did all they could to make it a success.

On the contrary, we are all familiar with follow-up books by famous authors, such as J.K. Rowling's first book for adults, *The Casual Vacancy* or *Twilight* author Stephanie Meyer's thriller *The Chemist*. They had all it normally takes, like a famous author, respected publishing house, media attention for the launch, etc. But after the initial interest, the books failed commercially.

The point I want to make here is that the strength of the manuscript, the raw power of the book, its inner beauty, is still the ultimate foundation for long term success.

---

[2] https://www.chickensoup.com/about/facts-and-figures

"The strength of the manuscript, the raw power of the story, the book's inner beauty, is still the ultimate foundation for a book's long term success."

When I say "the book is the star" I am not just referring to the manuscript, however, but also the 7 book marketing keys that you will learn in Chapter 2. It's the whole package you see when finding a book online or holding it in your hand physically in a bookstore, friend's house, or library.

Secret #1 is the most important secret, as it is so fundamental to an author's or publisher's mindset. But in order to understand what a fantastic book is, how it is described and can be spotted, we will have to give much more meat to it. Using a term like "fantastic book" without giving it any substance is too vague for actionability. The true question is how an author or publisher can make a book fantastic and what he/she needs to focus on.

The three main questions that need to be answered are:

1) *How do we spot a funtastic book, and what are the metrics?*

2) *What are the areas a publisher needs to work on?*

3) *How can a book be tested and improved in order to become fantastic?*

You will find the answers to these questions in detail throughout this book. For now, though, I want to give a quick overview to lay the groundwork.

1) *How do we spot a fantastic book? What are the metrics?*

There is only one metric that truly counts: customer satisfaction. A fantastic book is loved by its target audience, has ratings that average at least above 80%, has conversion rates of 10%+, and ideally achieves some form of organic growth or even virality with little or no advertising expense.

2) *What are the areas a publisher needs to work on?*

There are 8 critical areas for book success: The book manuscript, and the 7 book marketing keys that you will learn more about in Chapter 2.

3) *How can a book be tested and improved in order to become fantastic?*

The method that I recommend is "lean book publishing." You will learn more about it in Secret #4. This is a process of developing or improving an existing book based on feedback and interactions with the target audience.

A fantastic book will make its own way in the world, once seen by enough targeted people. You will learn about this in Secret #5.

Ultimately, "the book is the star" (Secret #1) is most importantly a mindset. It means a focus on creating a fantastic book, a book that is loved by readers and a book that the author can be proud of. A book that has the power to leave a legacy.

📖 Secret #1 Checkbox

📝 Core Insights:

✓ Having a strong book is still the best foundation for long-term book success

✓ Strong books enjoy high levels of customer ratings

✓ Investments into your book pay off more than investments into marketing and advertising

🎛 Exercise: Take the "Book Awesomeness Test"

Answer the following three questions. The more you answer "Yes," the further you are in your journey. The more you answer "No," the more room you have for improvement.

1) Does my book have the metrics of a fantastic book?

2) Do I know more than 10 readers who really loved my book?

3) What is my honest answer to the question: "Is my book amazing?"

Read on to learn how to get more "Yes" and how to make your book fantastic.

2

⚷ The 7 Book Marketing Keys

"Give me a bad manuscript, and by polishing it with the 7 keys to book marketing success, I will still make it sell."

"Give me a bad manuscript, and by polishing it with the 7 keys to book marketing success, I will still make it sell."

This sounds like a pretty bold statement, but I have seen it numerous times: good marketers can make a bad-to-average manuscript sell well, simply by improving the 7 book marketing keys. And of course, the improvement of the 7 keys is also one of the most important jobs that I do in my daily practice working with authors and publishers.

Changing and improving a manuscript is often difficult or almost impossible, especially for fiction books once they are on the market and have reached critical mass and circulation. That's why marketers

25

often have to turn exclusively to the 7 keys, which you will find out about in this chapter. Hold on tight, here they are:

The 7 Book Marketing Keys	
Key 1	Book Cover
Key 2	Book Title [+subtitle]
Key 3	Book Description
Key 4	Book Layout
Key 5	Author and Publisher
Key 6	Reviews [editorial, consumer]
Key 7	Marketing Strategy

Key 1: Book Cover

We all know the saying, "Don't judge a book by its cover," and we all know that it is impossible. We see the cover first before we ever get the chance to read a book. There is no way around it. And it has not changed with digital publishing, either. A book cover is the face of a book. Even more, it's really the whole body. Analytics have shown that good covers can increase Click-Through Rates by a couple of hundred percent[3], as well as decide whether a book becomes a commercial success or not. Saving your budget with the cover is one of the worst things you can do. You have to get the cover right.

Christiana Miller from *Self-Publishing On A Shoe String* says it well: "A book cover is an invitation — a way of seducing the reader. It beckons, inviting them to enter the world of your book and dance with your characters for awhile. It makes a promise about what kind of music they'll be dancing to. Your cover should convey the tone and genre of your story, be eye-catching and, most importantly, look like it's been professionally done."[4]

Creating beautiful and commercially successful covers is a topic with enough meat to write a whole book about it all on its own, so I do not want to dive too deep. Nevertheless I want to share with you the "formula" that I use when creating or assessing client covers, so you can use it for yourself.

---

[3] https://en.99designs.at/blog/tips/impact-book-cover-design-on-sales/
[4] https://www.huffpost.com/entry/selfpublishing-on-a-shoes_2_b_4325962

The cornerstone of my formula is the concept of "genre matching"[5] which I see as one of the most useful and simple concepts for creating commercially successful covers. The basic idea is to look at bestselling books in the relevant genre and to match book covers accordingly with respect to the overall styles. Just by matching core styles (such as typography, visuals, etc.) you not only match reader's expectations but also automatically match key selling factors in specific genres, such as the importance of looking fresh and up-to-date in the field of "how-to" books, or dreamy and warm with romance novels.

The second and third parts of my formula relate to communicating benefits and matching book title and visuals. Ideally, the book title already contains the core benefit. If not, I recommend using the subtitle on the cover as well. What's often overlooked, but also critical, is to match the title with the visual. If you have a book title that says *Book Sales Explosion* (one of my upcoming books) and you do not add a visual that looks explosive, you will not properly communicate

---

[5] https://blog.flipsnack.com/how-to-design-a-book-cover-based-on-its-genre/

your title. It is important that both title and visual click, that they are symbiotic.

Nevertheless, genre-matching, title/visual matching, and benefit communication are not enough. Even with these, you won't necessarily stand out. And book publishing is so competitive that you have to stand out. You need to catch the reader's attention as he browses through the list on Amazon or walks through a book store. Just take a look at the book cover of Donna Tartt's *The Goldfinch: A Novel*[6] and you will understand what I mean.

---

[6] https://www.amazon.com/dp/B00BAXFECK

Look inside ↓

▶ Audible Sample

© *Screenshot of Amazon - Nov 11, 2019*

That's why the cover formula that I apply contains "adding unique twists" as well, elements that are out of the ordinary. This in the book cover formula you see below, which I use with my clients.

Book Cover Formula:

Genre Match + Title/Visual Match + Benefits + Unique Twists = Wow Effect

Let's look at the cover of this book and apply the formula to it.

It matches the genre of "book marketing educational books" (advice and how-to), the visual "magic book" matches the book title *Book Marketing Secrets*, the title includes the core benefit, and the unique twist is the simplicity. It catches my eye, and I am happy with it. For me, the cover gets 4x yes, which brings the desired wow effect.

Could it be better? Yes, it always can. But based on my XP, this is a solid book cover. Apply the book cover formula for your own covers and put the formula to the test. I would be happy to hear your results.

Book Cover Formula Check: Book Marketing Secrets	
	Genre matching: yes Title/Visual match: yes Benefits communicated: yes Unique twist: yes ——————— Resulting wow effect: yes

Apply the formula to your own book covers and see how well they perform.

Key 2: Book Title

The second book marketing key is the book title. Over the years, I've created a formula that helps me to check for the main characteristics in book titles, to make sure that my clients' titles work. The formula calculates the score of the strength of four characteristics (0-25 points) to reach a total score between 0 and 100 points (100 points being the top value) The simplified version, which we will use now, gives either a Yes or a No to achieving a characteristic, with 4 Yes answers as the highest score. You can see the formula below.

Magic Book Title Formula	
<u>Characteristic</u>	<u>Count or Y/N</u>
Short and Memorable (easy to read, easy to pronounce, easy to listen to)	0-25 (Y/N)
Unique and Attention Grabbing (immediately engages emotions)	0-25 (Y/N)
Story Match (theme, cover, tone, content)	0-25 (Y/N)

Built-In Benefit	0-25 (Y/N)
Total Score	0-100 (X/Yes)

Books that achieve scores between 90-100 points, or alternatively 4 Yes answers, pass my assessment. All titles that are below 90 points, or with 3 Yes answers or lower, are candidates for improvement.

Let's take a closer look at the characteristics by looking at three popular best-selling book titles. These also share one common trait: they have exceptionally well-crafted, high-performing book titles, created by publishing professionals who understand their art superbly. These are superb book titles that we can learn from.

The titles I have chosen are the thriller *Blue Moon: A Jack Reacher Novel*[7] by Lee Child, the book *The Goldfinch: A Novel* (Pulitzer Prize for Fiction)[8] and the book *Educated: A Memoir*[9] by Tara Westover.

---

[7] https://www.amazon.com/Blue-Moon-Jack-Reacher-Novel-ebook/dp/B07NCNVZ5P

[8] https://www.amazon.com/dp/B00BAXFECK

[9] https://www.amazon.com/dp/B072BLVM83

Let's do a quick check and see why these titles are performing so well. First of all, they are all short and memorable. This is even with the added subtitle, as presented in my examples and as displayed in online book stores.[10] They are easy to read, easy to pronounce, and easy to listen to. They are also all unique and attention grabbing, and immediately engage the emotions. This is especially true for *Blue Moon*, which on an unconscious level immediately draws us to the book, because of the unique combination of the color and the object, combined with the ease of sound.

But most importantly, all of these titles have built-in benefits, even although none of the titles are "how to" or a typical non-fiction book.[11] The built-in benefits are easily recognizable in the subtitle (price winner, category, brand name). However, what's more remarkable is that the built-in benefits are also to a

---

[10] For digital book sales, subtitles get added to include important SEO-relevant keywords, such as the category, as well as important purchase factors, such as an award or prize, as shown in the example for *The Goldfinch*.

[11] *Educated: A Memoir* is a work of art in non-fiction, but is nevertheless close to fiction. That's why, for illustration purposes, it is not described as a typical non-fiction book, such as cookbooks, advice books, etc.

good extent communicated through the core titles themselves. In *Educated* the benefit is very clear, as it appeals to an educated target audience. The other two titles are more subtle, but they do their job as well. They draw readers into their stories due to the excellent match of title and story/theme.

Now it's your turn. I invite you to take a look at your book titles and apply the "magic book title formula" to them. How well do your titles perform? What can you do to improve them?[12]

---

[12] Even if your book is already published and you can no longer edit the title (for print versions), most digital publishing platforms allow you to at least edit the subtitle, which can be used to communicate benefits and improve scores of the four characteristics described.

> -> Check your book titles and see how many times they receive a "Yes"
>
> -> What can you do to improve your book title/subtitle?

Key 3: Book Description

Bestselling author Sarah Gribbles gets it right when she says: "Your book description isn't a summary of your book — it's an ad meant to hook your readers and sell your book."[13]

Having a powerful book description is a key element in book marketing. The main point is to get targeted readers to purchase the book. It is as simple as that. The details change depending on whether you create descriptions for fiction or non-fiction, for different genres and topics, as well as formats and places the descriptions appear, such as the back cover, an Amazon sales page, a PR text, or a newsletter. However, the core elements you need to master and

---

[13] Source: Sarah Gribble, https://thewritepractice.com/how-to-write-a-book-description/

communicate are the same. I want to share these critical elements with you and present you a powerful toolbox that not only helps you to craft powerful descriptions, but also to check them for effectiveness.

The following toolbox gives you six tools that I like to work with when creating and assessing book descriptions. The first four tools are process-oriented, which means you can use these tools to create your descriptions from scratch.

The latter two are ingredients you add in order to spice up your description and also test your descriptions for effectiveness. I will briefly explain each tool.

Let's start with the first four tools. I recommend that you rely on only one of these core tools for each description you create, as this keeps complexity low.

The first tool is the "Scribe Book Description Writing Method for Non-Fiction Books"[14], which shows how to hook readers, how to create pain and pleasure, legitimacy, and an open loop as a closing. It's a solid

---

[14] Source: Scribe Writing https://scribewriting.com/write-book-description/

method that you can learn more about by visiting the Scribe website (see footnote).

Another great method is to answer the "Who, Why, What & How" questions in your description, as Russell Brunson suggests for creating short but powerful video messages. This method is especially useful for authors who already have credibility in a certain area (Who), as the method suggests starting with the introduction of the author.

A technique that I like a lot is the one I created specifically for non-fiction books: use a great first sentence to "hook" readers, explain what the book is about in the next two sentences or "blurb," followed by "benefits" (presented in bullets), and close with a strong call-to-action (CTA).

Finally, the well-known AIDA model[15] can be applied excellently to book descriptions as well, in order to move readers step-by-step from attention, to interest, to desire, to action.

_____

[15] Source: Wikipedia
https://en.wikipedia.org/wiki/AIDA_(marketing)

Book Description Creation Toolbox*	
*outcomes to be assessed from reader's perspective	
Tool	Description
Scribe Book Description Writing Method for Non-Fiction Books	"Hook, Pain, Pleasure, Legitimacy, Open Loop"
Russell Brunson Intro Format	Who, Why, What, How
Albert's Non-Fiction Technique	Hook, Blurb, Benefits (bullets) + CTA
AIDA Technique	Attention, Interest, Desire, Action
Cialdini Principles	6 Principles of Persuasion (7th principle added in 2016)
Reader's Perspective Cooking Tools	-> Use "you" -> Use SEO keywords -> Use power verbs -> Active and present

One of my favorite ingredients for spicing up any book description come from well-known psychologist Robert Cialdini. His classic book on persuasion and influence[16] describes 6 principles, which you can use like spices in your book description "dish." The 6 principles (a 7th principle, "unity," was added in 2016) are reciprocity, consistency, social proof, liking, authority, and scarcity. I personally use these principles like salt and pepper throughout my own marketing. They are a powerful arsenal for every marketer. Concrete applications include: "Bestselling author, read by XY people, award-winning, limited bonus offer, etc." I recommend that you make sure that your book description covers all these principles in some form, for best results. Closing book descriptions with scarcity works especially well (eg. bonus offer inside the book is only available for first 1K readers, limited book edition, or introductory price), as this kind of scarcity is rarely used for books in general.

Finally, the sixth tool is all about writing and checking your book description from the reader's perspective. You have to make sure that your prospective reader understands what is in it for them. Enter the mind of

---

[16] Source: Robert Cialdini. *Influence: The Psychology of Persuasion* (1984) https://www.amazon.com/Influence-Psychology-Persuasion-Robert-Cialdini/dp/006124189X

the prospective reader and read the descriptions from their perspective.

The four core elements I suggest you look at are the use of the verb "you" in order to communicate with the reader (eg. You will learn, your best read of the year, etc.), the use of "power verbs"[17] (such as because, exclusive, quick, simple, etc.), "active voice"[18] and "present tense,"[19] and keywords that your readers will actively look for (especially by typing them into search engines). Once you know exactly what terms your readers are looking for, you can use them in your copy. Not only does this help you be found and rank higher, but also reminds your readers why they were looking for your book as they read your description.

The following chart shows why it is so important to rank as number 1 for specific keywords. You will get

---

[17] Source: Copy Write Matters
https://copywritematters.com/copywriter-words-that-sell/

[18] Source: Crazy Egg https://www.crazyegg.com/blog/double-power-of-content/

[19] Source: Susan Green
https://www.susangreenecopywriter.com/articles/write-website-content.html

27%[20] of all clicks for a keyword on Amazon, and data for other search engines is similar. Ranking high for your reader's search terms is an important aspect to consider when writing your book description.

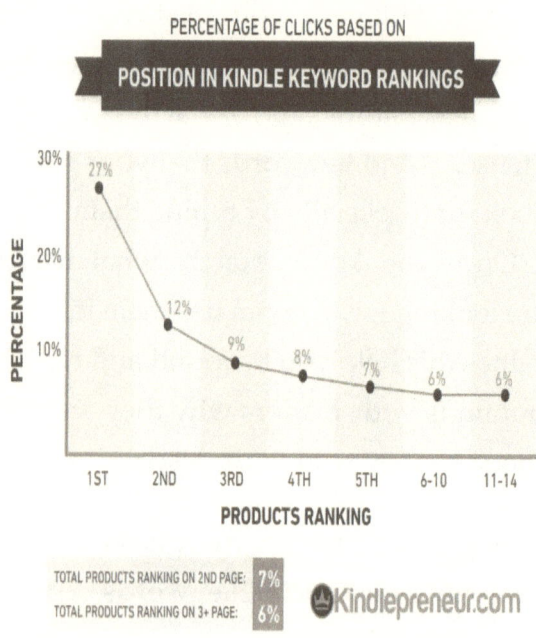

Source: https://kindlepreneur.com/how-to-choose-kindle-keywords/

---

[20] Source: Kindlepreneur: https://kindlepreneur.com/how-to-choose-kindle-keywords/

> ꝏꝏ The 7 Book Marketing Keys |
> Exercise 3 (Description)

> -> Pick one of the tools of the "Book Description Creation Toolbox" and start to write a description for an upcoming book project you have in mind.
>
> -> Check if your book descriptions apply some of "Cialdini's Principles" as well as the "Reader's Perspective Cooking Tools."

4) Book Layout

The next book marketing key is the book layout. This refers to how well the book is formatted, which influences the experience a reader has when reading your book, both as a paperback and as an ebook. Of particular importance for us are typography, images, and the use of quality elements like drop caps, breakout boxes, sidebars, contents, the first pages of the book, and the absence of typos, widows, and orphans.

Experienced publishers know that a good layout makes a huge difference in the perception of a book. However, layout is often not treated as importantly as it should be. In my experience, improving the layout is often a quick win, especially compared to re-writing manuscripts. Investing in a good formatter usually pays off, especially in the area of "advice and how-to." In this genre, authors can achieve a lot by investing in well-designed content, breakout or takeaway boxes, as well as chapter summaries and checklists.

In the following you'll find a table showing important elements to add to and improve your book layout, in order to increase the positive perception of your book:

Important Book Layout Factors	
Non-Fiction	Fiction
Typography (fonts, typeface, line height, font-size, drop caps, sinks, whitespace)	Typography (fonts, typeface, line height, font-size, drop caps, sinks, whitespace)
Use of Images/Illustrations	Use of Images/Illustrations
Nicely Designed Content	Nicely Designed Content
Margins, running heads, page numbers	Margins, running heads, page numbers
Absence of typos, widows, and orphans	Absence of typos, widows, and orphans

Use of breakout boxes, chapter summaries, infographics, sidebars	
Use of references, like footnotes, sources, indexes, links	

One element I want to draw your attention to in particular is the very beginning of the book, namely the first couple of pages. They are especially important online, as retailers allow readers to look at your first pages and get a reading sample for free. We all know Amazon's "Look Inside" feature. Optimizing your beginning pages can have a profound impact on your book sales, not to mention your publishing business as a whole. Why? I will explain that in a second.

So, first of all, it is important to understand that almost every Amazon reader uses the "Look Inside" function before purchasing a book[21]. That means that not only people who eventually purchase your book take a

---

[21] As I did not find data on this, I did a quick online survey with 10 respondents, where 8 out of 10 respondents said that they always use "Look Inside" before purchasing a book on Amazon.

look, but also all prospects (often 10x more than actual buyers).

Smart marketers understood that and started to not only optimize their "Look Inside" in order to get more readers, but also to market other services and to drive people to their websites, as readers can click on links within "Look Inside" to open external webpages as well.

One of my favorite uses of "Look Inside" is the "surprise gift"[22] or "added bonus content." The basic idea is to communicate visually striking bonus content within the first couple of pages (normally before the actual content), in order to give people added value to the book purchase. This also presents non-readers with an offer on your webpage as well, ideally accessible by signing up with their email. By following this approach, you are able to build email lists much faster and in a very targeted way.

Investing in a good book layout pays off. It's also mentioned as a quality factor from reviewers in 15%

---

[22] You can learn more about my surprise gift application by taking a look at this presentation:
https://www.slideshare.net/griesmayr/how-to-get-book-reviews-2020-edition

of reviews for non-fiction and 5% of reviews for fiction books[23], as my team and I found out in a study of 500 top reviews analyzed on Amazon. I will talk more about that when we look at Secret #6.

⌗ The 7 Book Marketing Keys |
Exercise 4 (Book Layout)

-> Take one of your most important books and make a list of layout elements that can be improved.

-> Read your book's reviews to see if any of them are referring to layout. If yes, take appropriate action, such as fixing typos or adding drop caps.

---

5) Author and Publisher

Another book marketing key is the perceived quality of the author and/or publisher. This key seems obvious, as books are linked to their authors and publishers through the whole branding experience. Still, in my practice working with authors and

---

[23] Data comes from a 2019 Scribando study that analyzed the contents of more than 500 Amazon reviews of 100 books, both in fiction and non-fiction.

publishers worldwide, I notice that especially the more inexperienced players significantly underestimate this book marketing key.

It is obvious that first-time authors often do not have a lot of credibility in the market and are shy to compete with big household names. However this should not lead to actions like practically hiding author names on book covers and book retailers. Not everything is about credibility. It's just as important to show readers who you are as well. A strong story can have such a profound effect on sales, it is vital that authors and publishers think deeply about how to present themselves in a favorable way.

You should definitely create a strong author biography. Explain who you are, why you wrote the book and why it's important, what is in the book, how your readers can purchase it, get the most out of it, connect with you, etc. You do not need to be rock star right out of the gate. A good story behind your book and why you wrote it can make up for a million sales. Include your author biography in your book, as well as online on your webpage and via online retailers. Very often the reason someone purchases a book, or why they don't, is because it really is "all about the author."

While the name of the publisher is less important, it still helps in most cases to be published with a respected publishing house (or at least not directly identified as "self-published"). Readers look for that information as well, in order to assess "credibility" and to reduce risk.

⸫ The 7 Book Marketing Keys I Exercise 5 (Author/Publisher)
-> Take a look at your author/publisher profiles on your webpage, Amazon, LinkedIn, etc., and make a list of elements you can improve. Think deeply about the reasons why you wrote the book (your story) and credibility factors you have. Improve your story and add credibility to your author biography.

6) Reviews

One of my favorite book marketing quotes is, "Reviews are the lifeblood of books in the digital age." Actually, how to get reviews is normally the #1 task that I discuss with my clients during my consulting sessions. A study by the Spiegel Research Center[24] in 2017 showed that 95% of buyers read online reviews before making a purchase. 95% - a very high number, but I am not surprised by that. Not only based on my personal experience (I always check reviews before purchasing a product), but also based on my experience with client books (books with bad average reviews are extremely difficult to market).

"Reviews are the lifeblood of books in the digital age."

So the task is obvious: having lots of good reviews is one of the most important book marketing keys to focus on, so it is best to start collecting them as early as possible. Simply said, there is no better time to start getting reviews than before having launched your book. This is especially important, as the first reviews set the tone for what's to come.

"The first reviews set the tone for what's to come."

---

[24] Source: Spiegel Research Center (2017):
https://spiegel.medill.northwestern.edu/_pdf/Spiegel_Online%20Review_eBook_Jun2017_FINAL.pdf

And the best way to get reviews early is to include potential readers, inviting them into your writing process as early as possible. Some call it their "launch team," others their "following," but in the end it's about engaging readers before actually launching your book. Not only to get "editorial reviews" from respected players in your field that you can use for your blurb and in your marketing, but also "customer reviews" that you can "activate"[25] when your book is launched.

I'll talk more about different ways to get reviews, including my favorite and most suggested methods, in a later secret. So I'll close this section for now. What's important is that you remember reviews are one of the most relevant book marketing keys, a factor that truly makes or breaks books.

---

[25] Most retailers do not allow posting reviews for books that are not released yet (eg. pre-order books). "Activation" refers to a process of securing a review from a reader through an ARC, and asking him to post the review once the book is available.

-> Take a look at the reviews your books have received. Rank them according to their average rating and rethink your book prioritization based on customer feedback.

-> Make sure that for upcoming book projects you make getting both editorial and customer ratings before book launch a priority and take appropriate action.

7) Marketing Strategy

Creating winning book marketing strategies is one of my core areas as a book marketing consultant. Over the last 10 years, I have created more than 100 book marketing strategies for clients from all over the world. In basic terms, a book marketing strategy is about providing a clear step-by-step action plan for how to reach the marketing-related author/publisher goal[26] within a predefined time frame and a given budget.

---

[26] In most cases the goal is to reach certain sales numbers, supported by sub-goals, like getting reviews.

The crucial question in most strategies is how to reach a substantial amount of targeted readers in the most cost-effective way. Marketing strategy is mostly about using the right channels with the right tactics and messages.

Book marketing strategies can be seen as stand-alone products. They have value regardless of the quality of the underlying book. However, every skilled marketer knows that each strategy is based on the power of the product, and success or failure greatly depend on that quality.

That's why it is no secret that every strategy will greatly benefit from a fantastic book and already-optimized book marketing keys as a foundation. Below, you'll find a simple "book marketing strategy creation cheat sheet" that includes 4 questions to answer to come up with a basic strategy.

By answering these 4 questions, you will already have made significant progress toward creating a winning strategy for your book. However, I recommend authors and publishers without much experience in book marketing to reach out to a book marketing expert for advice in this important strategic area.

Book Marketing Strategy Creation Cheat Sheet
1. What is the goal I want to reach? (eg. sales numbers)
2. Who are my perfect readers? Who likes my book?
3. How many people do I need to reach? (to reach my goal)
4. What are the channels I have to use? (to reach my audience)
5. How good does my product need to be? (to reach my goal)

Having the right strategy means being able to do the right things from the start, which results in dollars invested the right way and increased chances for success.

⌗ The 7 Book Marketing Keys I Exercise 7 (Book Marketing Strategy)
-> Take a book you are marketing right now, and answer the 5 questions in the "Book Marketing Creation Cheat Sheet."

By mastering the 7 book marketing keys, you will be able to reach targeted readers with a product that they will buy.

Once you have achieved this, it really comes down to your manuscript and the inner power and beauty of your book. Master book marketing Secret #1 (the book is the star) together with #2 (the 7 book marketing keys), and you will have everything you need to create a true bestseller.

📖 **Secret #2 Checkbox**
Core Insights:
✓ Master the 7 book marketing keys, and be able to sell solid books with ease
✓ Know the 7 book marketing keys by heart and optimize them relentlessly

⚎ Exercises

Get pen and paper and take notes:

1. List the 7 book marketing keys

2. Which of the 7 keys can be improved for your book?

3. Make a list of steps to improve your 7 keys by doing the 7 exercises described in this chapter

⬕ The 80/20 Rule Of Book Marketing

I still remember when I first heard about the Pareto Principle, also referred to as the 80/20 rule. It was back in university, when I was a student at the University of Economics and Business Administration in Vienna, taking a basic class in economics. It puzzled me when the professor said that, for many events in economy and life, roughly 80% of the effects come from 20% of the causes.[27]

The professor talked about wealth distribution and business processes, as well as personal finances. It was the first time that I'd heard of the 80/20 rule and was one of the main principles I learned at university that really stuck with me. Over the years to come, I learned

---

[27] Source: Wikipedia:
https://en.wikipedia.org/wiki/Pareto_principle

what a great rule it was and the many practical applications it had.

So, years later, when I started to consult for authors, I started to wonder whether the rule was true for book marketing as well. Do 80% of royalties, or in a broader context book sales, come from only 20% of efforts? Do publishing houses have 1 winner out of 5 that covers the marketing expenses of all others?

So I dug deeper and found out that the Pareto Principle was also valid for a lot of relationships in book publishing. When analyzing client projects, I found that it was often only one particular sales channel that brought income, and one good book that really sold.

What struck me the most, though, was that I figured out that the rule applies to other aspects as well which are quite unique for books. And those other aspects are the following:

The 80/20 Rule Of Book Marketing
[3 Underlying Facts]

1) 20% effort brings 80% outcome

2) 80%+ is invested into the manuscript, but only 1%-20% is invested in the 7 book marketing keys

3) But 80% importance is in book keys when purchasers make a buying decision

So let's take a closer look at the second and third application of the secret. The second application says:

80%+ of time/effort is invested into manuscript, but only 1%-20% is invested into the 7 book marketing keys

If you are a true author (and not a publisher only hiring ghostwriters) you will most certainly agree with me on this. The huge effort is writing the book itself, filling the story, putting it all together, editing it, etc. The effort put into the 7 book marketing keys, though, is way less. We often take this even as a byproduct of finishing a book. This is especially true if we start out with just the manuscript and add on the 7 keys at the end of the process. Then we are often already out of energy or even funds. We just can't wait to see our baby on the shelves and online.

However, what we learned in Secret #2 is that around 80% of your success depend on the 7 book marketing keys. The 7 book marketing keys which we only give attention and resources to for around 20% of our time.

So we see that something is wrong here. Most of us are investing too much time into something that does not bring much of an outcome. Or, what's even worse, into something that might never be discovered, if your 7 book marketing keys are not convincing. You could have an amazing book, but with average book marketing keys, you will lose a lot of ground or might not even make it past the first reader.

So I suggest you take the following two insights from the facts above:

1) Find the 20% of effort that brings 80% of results and focus on them.
2) And join me for an experiment: Why not do it the other way round and invest 80% of resources into the 7 book keys, and only 20% into the manuscript?

That sounds crazy, right? Impossible. But it isn't. And that's why it is so powerful. In a second I will show you how it works, where it works, and why it works so well.

I invite you to enter the world of "zero or low content book publishing."

It is a world in which the focus is on creating books with minimum effort but maximum outcome. Books that have zero or low content (easy-to-create manuscripts), while on the other hand are driven by their 7 book marketing keys.

Notebooks and creative books, summaries, quote books, etc., all brought down to their essentials. Some of the publishers in this market are there for the quick book. So not all of them pay attention to the 7 keys. But there a couple of great publishers who are masters in their field, and that results in truly amazing book projects.

Two examples I want to share with you. One is *The Little Notebook For Big Ideas*[28] by Rob Cubbon. Another is *Writers Block*[29] by me.

---

[28] Source: https://www.amazon.com/LITTLE-NOTEBOOK-Motivational-Journal-Entrepreneurs/dp/1724026372

[29] Source: https://www.amazon.com/Writers-Block-What-feels-about-ebook/dp/B00NVKDT68/

These are great projects that apply the 80/20 rule of book marketing and show what is possible by focusing on the 7 book marketing keys at first. Do they match the criteria because their manuscripts are so thin? Yes, that's true. So they are not 100% representative. But I am sharing those to inspire you and to ask you a question:

"What would be possible with your book projects if you invested 80% of your efforts into the 7 book marketing keys instead of your manuscripts? What would happen if you started to focus on those first, before finishing your manuscript?"

> *"What would be possible with your book projects if you invested 80% of your efforts into the 7 book marketing keys instead of your manuscripts?"*

I believe that we have already entered an era of book publishing in which the focus shifts dramatically away from the manuscript to the 7 book marketing keys. We are already seeing the change today: business-oriented market entrants such as Kindle Publishing are competing on Amazon daily, SEO is critical, book editors and translators are supported and threatened at the same time by technology doing their job, the growing demand for audio brings formats[30] that reduce production times significantly, and speech-to-text technology enables faster ways to produce manuscripts.

Digital marketing knowledge has become paramount in an increasingly competitive and global technology driven market. Not all of these developments are rosy.

And what's more, we are on the brink of a new era. An era that not many see yet, but which I believe is close. The era of "artificial intelligence" in book publishing. We are writing late 2019, and AI regarding the creation of books is still in its very early stages. However, given the rate of development and adoption of technological advances in the last decades, it is only reasonable to assume that AI will literally write books faster than we can dream of today.

"AI will literally write books faster than we can dream of today."

As a result, AI will create a book publishing landscape in which the resources invested in the 7 book marketing keys vs. the manuscript will have changed

---

[30] Formats such as audiobooks, CDs, or Alexa Skills. [Time of writing: October 2019]

dramatically. AI will literally write book publishing history. Today is the best day to start to invest big time into the 7 book marketing keys (Secret #2) and to apply the 80/20 rule of book marketing to your advantage.

The 80/20 Rule Of Book Marketing [2 To-Dos]

1) Find the 20% effort that brings 80% outcome and focus on it
2) Invest at least 20% (or, better, 50%) of your resources into the 7 book marketing keys

My rule of thumb and core recommendation is that you not only give the 7 book marketing keys the same importance as your manuscript right from the beginning of your book project, but that you also spend at least 20% (but better 50% or more) of your resources on those 7 keys, in order to make your book a success.

 **Secret #3 Checkbox**

Core Insights:

✓ 20% effort brings 80% outcome

✓ 80%+ is invested in manuscript, but only 1%-20% is invested in the 7 book marketing keys

✓ But 80% importance is in book keys, when purchasers make a buying decision

Exercises

Take pen and paper and answer the following questions:

1) -What is your 20% that brings 80% of results?

2) -Did you invest at least 20% of your time in the 7 book marketing keys?

3) -What are low-hanging fruits [tasks with low effort/big outcome ratio] you can grab now to improve your book sales?

4

🏃 The Power Of Lean Book Publishing

When I started my book publishing company Scribando | Novelify in 2012, there was one concept *en vogue* in the world of internet startups. This concept was "The Lean Startup" by Eric Ries.[31]

The corresponding book was published in 2011 and quickly became a bestseller in the business field and, ultimately, even a New York Times bestseller. Every small company wanted to become lean, more efficient, and reduce the risk of failure by being more customer-centric.

The lean startup movement was huge, and swept across startup hubs globally in no time. Eric Ries was right, and he still is. Applying lean startup principles is

---

[31] Source and further information: http://theleanstartup.com/

profoundly the right way in order to achieve product-market fit quickly, as many successful technology companies born during that time, such as Dropbox, Wealthfront, or Airbnb, showed in later years.

I applied lean principles in my company as well, and was able to innovate quickly. Not everything turned out to be successful. What I learned was that being in touch with your customers from the early stage onwards helps you to find product-market fit way more quickly.

Soon I started to wonder whether lean principles would also be useful for the process of book publishing. I quickly learned that authors such as Guy Kawasaki, Aaron Hurst, Ksenia Anske, and Paulo Coelho, and publishers such as O'Reilly were experimenting with lean startup principles. New publishing platforms like Leanpub and the now-closed Pubslush were providing ways for publishers to write and publish the lean way.

I felt the need of a knowledge resource about lean publishing, and so I registered the domain www.leanbookpublishing.com, created presentations sharing principles and insights, and uploaded them onto the website. I talked to authors, shared knowledge, and even presented Lean Book

Publishing at a Pecha Kucha Night. It was an inspiring time. The webpage and concept is still online and, more importantly, more valid than ever today.

> "The core idea of lean book publishing is to publish books readers love and to find out what works and what doesn't as quickly and cost-efficiently as possible. That is what Lean Book Publishing is about at its core."
>
> Visit www.leanbookpublishing.com to learn about the principles, tools, and benefits of lean book publishing.

Little has changed regarding the core concepts. What has evolved, though, are the tools that we have access to in 2019, around 7 years later. Almost everyone today can use social media and blogging platforms to test ideas or to find audiences for publishing and launch teams. Authors are way more familiar with technology, as well, and the share of authors who have webpages has grown drastically, too.

Testing book ideas, finding the right audiences for a book, as well as "sequential publishing," are now easier than ever, due to communities like Wattpad, private groups on Facebook, and easy access to book publishing tools, like Amazon's KDP. Still, the concept of lean book publishing did not celebrate a huge success.

So why is that? There are 2 questions emerging:

1) Did applying lean startup principles simple not make publishers and authors successful? or

2) Do not enough authors know about the concept?

Let's take a closer look at the answers. I want to start with looking at the historic development of the book publishing landscape, as well as the current iteration. Historically, writing books has always been a very private process. We all have the image in mind of authors sitting - separated from the world - in dimly lit work rooms, writing their book until, after years of hard work, it is done and can see the light.

Many of the best books ever created, have been created by writers in very isolated situations, deep inside their own brains. And most books, I would assume around 90%[32], are still primarily written this way, with little or

---

[32] Estimated number that is based on my personal work with more than 100 authors worldwide.

no interaction with others before the manuscript is finished. Following the writing process like this seems very much ingrained to us, which makes it difficult to change. Writing a book is still something very personal, a treasure that we as authors guard in our heart, a treasure that is very vulnerable in its making. It seems that this is a major reason why "lean publishing" has not yet found wide adoption.

So even if lots of authors and publishers knew about "lean book publishing," it still seems somewhat counterintuitive to apply it. What's more, we as authors sometimes fear copyright problems, or are overly confident about our writing as well. We all believe we have a great book in the making - if not a bestseller - otherwise we would not devote that much time to writing a book.

"Writing a book is still something very private. It's like a vulnerable treasure in the making that we as authors guard in our heart."

And frankly, bestselling authors like Stephen King, Scott Westerfeld, or John Grisham, as well as big publishing houses, like Random House, Simon & Schuster, and Hachette, will not want to rely on communities to give feedback on chapters, or even co-write whole books, simply because they have learned that they are able to publish bestsellers with their own expertise alone.

And this makes a lot of sense. It has worked in the past and still works like this to a large extent for experienced professionals. For others, though, it very often doesn't, mostly because they lack the professional experience to know what is needed to succeed in this competitive market. For unexperienced professionals, applying "Lean Book Publishing Principles" can not only drastically improve product-market fit, but also save months of work and substantial amounts of money.

Let's go back once more to the initial question, why LBP is still not as widespread as the lean concept is in other industries. Let's take a closer look at success stories, and go on an expedition to the largest writing community today, Wattpad, which has an audience of more than 70 million readers[33]. Wattpad, at its core, is a lean publishing platform. It enables writers to share their stories with readers during the writing process,

---

[33] https://en.wikipedia.org/wiki/Wattpad

to get feedback, and to grow fanbases long before books actually get published.

On such a big platform like Wattpad, we have to be able to find successful authors, right?

Yes, we do. We not only find thousands of authors who use Wattpad on a daily or weekly basis to connect with their readers and to generate consistent sales from their books, we also find authors who sold millions of copies[34] and got published by Big 5 publishing houses, such as NYT bestselling author Anna Todd[35] , the well-known author of the *After* series, who even sold the rights to Paramount Pictures for a movie adaptation[36]. Read what Anna says about Wattpad:

"I found Wattpad through reading fanfiction and from the second I laid my eyes on the platform, I fell down the rabbit hole. It was a place I couldn't have even dreamed existed with people just like me, an entire world of people who read and write on the internet. I found a community, a home really,

---

[34] Source: https://publishingperspectives.com/2017/11/anna-todd-foreign-rights-sales-wattpad-rights-edition/

[35] http://www.annatodd.com/

[36] Source: https://deadline.com/2014/10/after-movie-rights-wattpad-book-anna-todd-paramount-852926/

with these people who were writing in the hours off of work, school, parenting, life, and I loved every second of it. And I wrote. And wrote. And wrote and then wrote some more. I couldn't stop!"[37]

For me the quote is a beautiful description of how rewarding lean book publishing can be on a personal level. Two other successful authors using Wattpad are Lilian Carmine[38], the author of the *Lost Boys* novels and Brittany Geragotelis[39], author of the young adult series *LIFE'S A WITCH*. Both authors have not only been able to build substantial fan bases on Wattpad, but have also secured publishing deals with well-established publishing houses. So, many authors on Wattpad prove that "lean book publishing" works.

But do we need a dedicated platform for "lean book publishing" at all anymore? The straightforward answer is no. Social networks like Facebook have features like dedicated groups, which could be a way

---

[37] Source: http://www.annatodd.com/my-story/

[38] Lilian Carmine:
https://www.penguin.co.uk/authors/1072451/lilian-carmine.html

[39] Brittany Geragotelis:
https://www.simonandschuster.com/authors/Brittany-Geragotelis/405274297

to lean publish and get feedback. Crowdfunding platforms like Kickstarter[40] have shown and still show outstanding potential for applying lean publishing successful. Just go to Kickstarter.com and search for projects like "Hello Ruby," "Masters of Anatomy," or "The Leader's Guide by Eric Ries," to see examples of very successful projects that used "lean publishing elements," such as getting feedback and finding followers early. These projects raised hundreds of thousands of dollars from ten thousands of supporters. A priceless support, often even before the first chapter is written.

Also, Amazon has a couple of built-in features for applying lean book publishing principles. In addition, authors and publishers have found ways to use Amazon in a way that allows them to publish quickly and align with the feedback of their target audience.

Let's take a closer look at what is possible with Amazon, as well as other direct publishing platforms like Kobo Writer Life. First of all, Amazon's KDP platform provides an interface that allows authors to

---

[40] Kickstarter (www.kickstarter.com) is an often overlooked channel that has a lot of potential for success for publishers and authors.

test variants of the 7 book marketing keys as well as the manuscript. This allows for adaptation on an ongoing basis and, with ebooks, almost instantly. Simply upload a different book cover, show a different book description, or present a new manuscript. With Amazon, you can do that by clicking a couple of buttons. Amazon's approval normally follows within a couple of hours as well, resulting in a great platform for testing elements quickly.

But what about the core idea of finding out if readers like your book quickly, by publishing raw ideas and first chapters? Amazon does not provide a way to do that. At least, that's what we assume at first sight.

But what you will learn now might surprise you. Because both fiction and non-fiction authors have found ways, often without knowing about the concepts behind it, to publish the lean way. And this with big success!

I invite you to take a look at the author profile of well-known British writer Mark Dawson[41]. He is the creator of the John Milton series.

---

[41] https://www.amazon.com/Mark-Dawson/e/B0034Q9BO8

For non-fiction low content and 10 instead of 50 rules and pdf downloads, do not write a 500 page book. Break it into 5-10 parts instead, whether it is fiction or non-fiction.

This has many benefits. Not only is it faster to put on the market and provide the option for quicker feedback, but also offers advantages like better visibility in Amazon search (because there are more keywords) and higher total sales (when adding up individual prices). And what's more, LBP through Amazon also reduces failure rates. Realizing that you've failed with part 1 of a series is much easier than with a whole series/book published at once. And finally, LBP is also in line with a trend. People have less time to read big books. They want instant gratification.

So, to sum up, LBP is more relevant than ever before, and has found its way into book publishing. It is, however, not noticed for the most part, and when it is, it's not described as LBP.

For you as an author and publisher, this does not really matter anyway. What matters for you is that you are aware of the advantages that applying lean publishing principles to your books have. By relying on Secret #4, you will not only reduce costly failure and find the right target audiences for your book faster, but more importantly get closer to publishing books that your readers will truly love.

There is a popular quote that says "starting is the hardest."[42] However, I would argue that with books "finishing strong" is the harder part. And lean book publishing provides a fantastic way to not only start quickly, but also to stay motivated through the often lengthy writing time. Most importantly, it helps you to finish strong, based on a good product with an already established fan base.

> *"Being able to finish strong is a powerful and rewarding skill for publishers and authors to master."*[43]

---

[42] Quote by Simon Sinnek. "The hardest part is starting. Once you get that out of the way, you'll find the rest of the way much easier."

[43] You will learn more about that skill throughout this book, mostly in Secrets 9 and 10.

Secret #4 Checkbox

Core Insights:

✓ LBP is all about creating books that readers truly love

✓ LBP reduces failure rates and is a win-win for both authors and readers

✓ LBP is everywhere (in launch teams, book series, ebook first launches, podcasts, etc.)

Exercises

1) How could you apply lean book publishing principles to your books?

2) Do you have a story in the making that you could publish the lean way? And if yes, what are possible actions?

5

⚛ The Importance Of 10,000 Readers [A Book Launch]

What I have learned from my experience working individually with hundreds of authors from all over the world is that around 50% of authors who come to me are not aware of two critical points when launching their books:

1) It needs a substantial amount of targeted readers (ideally aiming for 10,000) that need to connect with your book, in order to give it a true chance for success

2) And secondly, it needs an investment into paid advertising and/or promotional campaigns in order to target these readers

Let's look at both points more closely.

The first point is constructed around a simplified calculation that is based on experience in the market. It says that if you manage to get around 10,000 targeted readers notified of your book launch (eg. via newsletter, high-quality online advertisement, radio, etc.) and convert 10%, to get 1,000 people on your book sales page (or in the physical world in touch with your book), you can expect around 10% to actually purchase your book, leaving you with 100 targeted readers, which are the minimum amount of readers needed to have given your book a true chance for success. If you continue the calculation with the simplified 10% conversion rate, you end up with only 10% of readers being an advocate[44], which means they give you feedback, spread the word, or write a review.

---

[44] "A brand **advocate** is someone who elevates your brand through word of mouth marketing. Brand **advocates** leave positive reviews about your **product**. They also refer new customers and create content on your behalf. Brand **advocates** even contribute useful insights to your user personas." Source: Sprout Social, 2019: https://sproutsocial.com/glossary/brand-advocate/

The Importance Of 10,000 Readers [Simple Calculation]		
Impressions	10K	10%
Sales Page	1K	10%
Readers	100	10%
Advocates	10	

Suddenly looking at a number of only 10 advocates or 100 readers, compared to the initial 10,000 people targeted, changes the perspective quickly. When also taking into account that 50% of books only get half read[45] and that having just a handful of brand advocates is seldom enough to trigger virality, we get closer to an understanding that in book marketing, as well as in digital product marketing as a whole, we need to target and think bigger numbers in order to reach critical mass.

Interestingly, we can learn the most in this respect from the book launches of successful online entrepreneurs and business owners. Just think of Peter

---

[45] Source: https://www.theifod.com/how-many-people-finish-books/

Voogd (founder of the Game Changer's Academy[46]), Sabri Suby (founder of King Kong[47]) or Russell Brunson (founder of Click Funnels[48]), who have successful online businesses and were able to apply their digital marketing knowledge of creating profitable paid advertising models to their book launches.

To give you a couple of numbers from their campaigns, Russell Brunson sold 66,000 books in 12 weeks in 2017[49], Peter Voogd earned $200,000 in royalties in 2 years from 2 books between 2016 and 2018[50], and Sabri Suby's book *Sell like Crazy*, launched in summer 2019, makes $10,000 on Amazon alone every month, just three months after launch[51].

I am not sharing these numbers to line up with the digital marketers out there screaming big numbers in

---

[46] Game Changer's Academy:
https://gamechangersmovement.com/

[47] Australian digital marketing agency: https://kingkong.com.au/

[48] US-American software company:
https://www.clickfunnels.com/

[49] Source: https://marketingsecrets.com/66k-books-sold/

[50] Information from Meanwhile Private Podcast

[51] Private research using paid software

order to create hype. No, I am sharing them to show you that sales numbers like this are possible for digital marketers, who are not coming from the book publishing industry and are not published by big publishing houses.

What these entrepreneurs do is to combine paid advertising (focusing on big numbers that go way beyond my recommended 10K+) with high-converting book sales funnels. And they apply a process that works over and over again.

By looking at entrepreneurs like this, we are able to more quickly change our thinking and to move away from the traditional and sometimes a little romantic book marketing model, in which we initially market our books to 10, 50 or 100 targeted persons and wait for the bestseller to happen.

For experienced digital marketers, these numbers are just ridiculously small. And for the sake of our books and the time, sweat, love, and effort we invested into them, we are wise to learn from them in this respect and apply "bigger numbers" thinking as well.

As a side note, I want to add that bigger publishing houses can also learn a lot from this thinking. Distribution is just different in the digital world. In bookstores publishers have the visibility for these basic numbers automatically, without giving it too much thought. But in the digital world, it is easy to overlook that the base distribution is often just not where it has to be in order to reach critical mass.

The second point I want to address is that it needs an investment in paid advertising and/or a launch campaign. This means allocating a budget for your book that allows you to pay for marketing campaigns reaching 10,000 targeted readers or more. And sometimes also for experts who are able to set up and monitor campaigns for you.

The truth is that you need to be prepared to invest the base amount needed [I suggest that this amount is at least $1,000 USD[52]] into paid advertising and/or promotional campaigns, in order to give your book a true chance to succeed.

---

[52] At the time of writing (Nov 2019) $1,000 USD is a good ballpark figure for the budget needed to reach 10K+ targeted readers through a book launch, by using email newsletter services or paid advertising campaigns. The expense includes advertising rates, as well as having a freelancer to help you with the basic setup if needed.

So when looking at the campaigns of publishing houses and digital marketers, we know what is necessary. But what does the reality look like? What do I see in the market when working with authors and publishers?

What I observe is that there is still a widespread assumption in the market that a good book will make its own way. Or that, once the book is uploaded to Amazon, it will get found in search and discovered.

This could not be further from the truth.

The fact is, if you upload a book on Amazon today, you can upload some random text, swear and do crazy things, and without marketing this book it is unlikely that someone will ever purchase it and discover what you did. At least that's true for new KDP accounts and first time authors. You want to give it a try? Do so. But of course, proceed at your own risk and be careful if you are an established author, publisher, or writing non-fiction based on clear user search intent. You might get caught.

The point I want to make clear is that without investing in having an audience to start with, you will not be able to get enough eyeballs on your book to give it a chance for success. You need to give your book a substantial push in the beginning. And I am not talking about a little nudge, like you give your kid the first time she goes sledding or rides a bike. No, I mean a substantial push out into the cold, out of your comfort zone, into new territory, so that you see if it stands and starts to thrive on its own.

Here is what I have developed as a rule of thumb over the last couple of years, consistent with the calculation shared at the beginning of this chapter: if you manage to reach 10,000 targeted prospects[53] through advertising and, out of them, around 1,000 highly-targeted readers visit your book sales page (eg. Amazon or personal book landing page), you get a lot of valuable data and feedback about conversion rates for your book marketing campaign.

And if you apply the calculation for your book launch and are able to convert 10% into readers who actually buy your book, you will not only get the base amount

------

[53] Key is the conversion rate, in order to get 1,000 highly targeted readers visiting your book sales page. The 10K work if they convert at 10%. To give you an example: In case you run display ad campaigns on Google, you will not manage a 10% conversion rate, you will need way more impressions. So in the end, the 10K work in case you are running high-quality ads with the right advertising method chosen.

of readers needed for proof-of-concept, but also start to be on a good track for creating profitable campaigns in the future. You will have given your book the chance it deserves for success. That's the secret of 10,000 readers.

"The calculation behind giving your book the chance for success is the secret of marketing to 10,000 readers."

But how much does it cost to reach 10K readers and to do a proper book launch?

From my experience, you do not need more than $1,000 USD[54] to do a basic book launch, including a paid advertising or email marketing campaign that reaches 10K+ targeted readers. Listing recommended campaigns at this point would go beyond the scope of this chapter, as well as doing calculations on CPCs for digital advertising campaigns, debating the suggested $1,000 ballpark figure, or going into details about my simplified 10% conversion rate, which will not hold up for many campaigns.

So I want to keep that short at this point. These are very simplified numbers, and will vary widely from book to

---

[54] At the time of writing in November 2019.

book and depending on the actual advertising or marketing campaign selected.

What's really important for me is to give you a simple and memorable recipe, based on my experience working on hundreds of book projects over the last couple of years. And that is what I am doing with the 10K reader secret.

Can the numbers be different? Yes, they can.

Do you need to invest $1,000 or more all at once, in order to push your book launch? No, you don't.

You can think lean and divide your advertising amount in 2-4 investment phases as well. This gives you the chance to learn from your campaigns and, ideally, also create revenue along the way to fund your expenses. You also don't need to invest everything into paid advertising services like AMS, Facebook, or Bookbub ads. There are also cheaper options to advertise and different ways to get eyeballs at lower cost. The opportunities are diverse and would go beyond the scope of this book, but just to name major areas, think about online PR, blogging, newsletter campaigns, collaborations with other authors, social media, etc.

As a first step, especially if your budget is limited and you need more feedback, you can also aim for at least 1,000 readers (ad impressions do not count, though). At a 10% conversion rate, you would get 100 readers, which is often the absolute minimum in order to create any form of virality and word-of-mouth or to have an effect on discoverability in Amazon search.

Are there exceptions to the rule?

Yes, most certainly. There will be exceptions, such as very targeted non-fiction books or truly amazing fiction books; however, you should not expect to be the exception. It's better to prepare for reality.

So ask yourself:

-> Did I give my book a real chance to succeed?

-> Did I invest enough money to get 10K readers (or as a minimum 1K readers) to my book sales page?

If you didn't and you believe in your book, come up with ways to get this exposure. Give your book the chance it deserves in the competitive landscape of book publishing.

Secret #5 Checkbox

Core Insights:

✓ Aim to reach at least 10K targeted readers (mere display ad impressions do not count, high-quality ads, mentions and interactions do), in order to give your book a chance for success

Exercises

1) Did you market your book to at least 10K targeted readers? If not, take appropriate action.

2) Did at least 100 targeted readers read your book? If not, take appropriate action.

6

⭐⭐ The One Factor Making Or Breaking Books

*T*here is one decisive factor that makes or breaks books: reviews. In the offline world, publishers are still able to keep the influence of reviews limited. But in the online world, reviews are almost everything. And this is supported by hard facts.

As already shared with you in Chapter 2, a study conducted by the Spiegel Research Center[55] in 2017 showed that 95% of buyers read online reviews before making a purchase. 95%. An incredibly high number, but I am not surprised.

Truth is, and I have seen it with clients numerous times, without a substantial amount of positive

---

[55] Source: Spiegel Research Center (2017):
https://spiegel.medill.northwestern.edu/_pdf/Spiegel_Online%20Review_eBook_Jun2017_FINAL.pdf

reviews, books will almost certainly die. Or, at the very least, not become very successful.

The basic rules regarding online reviews are:

Basic Rules Regarding Book Reviews

1) No reviews = No sales

2) The more reviews -> The more sales

3) The more positive reviews -> The higher the conversion rates, and the other way around

I am still surprised how often authors approach me with books that have 0 reviews and wonder why they have no sales. The first thing I always tell them is that the reason no one buys their book is because it has no reviews. Getting this external validation from an expert is often an eye-opener. That's the point when they realize that they absolutely need to fix this one problem first, before doing anything else.

And yes, if the book is good, your first step is to get 10 reviews for it, so that you can rise from the ashes.

For well-established authors and big publishers, getting the first 10-25 reviews is comparably easy. Just put together a proper book launch and inform the author's previous readers about the new book.

For first-time authors, self-published authors, and small publishers, however, the task of getting the first 5-25 reviews is difficult. And it does not get easier with Amazon's strict terms and community guidelines, prohibiting asking family, friends, and business associates, and not allowing to you to offer anything in return for the review.

For market players who want to do everything correctly, developments regarding online reviews have become a true burden. And I do not exclude myself here. Getting the first 25 reviews and doing everything properly and correctly is one of the most critical results that I have to achieve for my clients.

Over the years I developed a fantastic strategy though. Authors and publishers can use this strategy to get reviews ethically and at very high conversion rates. I call the strategy the "surprise gift strategy." It uses the "Look Inside" pages of a book to communicate the offer for a surprise gift that readers can access on the author's or publisher's webpage. After signing up with their email address, they get bonus content and also a request for feedback and a review.

When done properly, this strategy not only increases the conversion rates of getting reviews substantially, it also creates email lists of readers at incredible speed. I also use this strategy with my books. You can go through the process to see how, and learn how I do it to build my list and to get reviews.

Once you have this strategy in place and create a decent list of readers, it gets easier and easier to promote book launches and to get those first critical reviews.

First-time authors just starting to apply the "surprise gift strategy," or authors publishing for a new target audience, will still need to make an initial push for reviews. For those clients, I mostly recommend that they work with selected ARC-services and/or to research power reviewers who are not only highly interested in the respective niche, but also frequently provide reviews. By approaching power reviewers correctly, authors and publishers are not only able to get more reviews, but also to establish powerful business relationships in their fields. You can learn more about my latest advice for getting reviews by visiting my personal website www.albertgriesmayr.com.

Another critical aspect regarding reviews is that, interestingly, the quantity of reviews is generally more important than the quality. Books that have garnered 100+ reviews on Amazon, for instance, communicate "proof of concept" and give readers security and social proof that the book is established in the market.

However, the threshold between a perception of overall positive ratings to a perception of overall negative ratings is thin and has to be monitored closely. On Amazon, the threshold is at a rating of 4.25. It is visually visible by the amount and the extent of stars filled. Below, I'll show you two book examples with a rating of 4.2 and a rating of 4.3. You can easily see that there is a big difference in the perception of these ratings, although the actual difference in quality is very small.

Star Rating above 4.25 (to 4.7)	Star Rating below 4.25 (to 3.8)	Star Rating below 3.75 (to 3.3)
★★★★☆ (128)	★★★★☆ (62)	★★★☆☆ (65)

As a rule of thumb, you should always aim for a rating of over 4.25 in order to sell well. If you are below this rating, your sales will suffer. Being in the range between 4.2. and 3.8 is still acceptable for some books (depending on the competition, the genre, etc.) as well. However, below 3.75, click-through rates, sales, and perception get ugly quickly.

But more importantly, you should not only look at the economic message overall ratings provide, but carefully read all reviews and take criticism in order to improve your book. This leads me to the hidden core message of Secret #6. When I say "reviews make or break books," I do not only refer to the economical side of it. I also refer to the important "feedback mechanism" that reviews provide, in order to literally "make a book."

It's absolutely eye-opening to read through the reviews of a book that has 50 or 100+ reviews, because they reviewers say so much about the book. They talk about the quality of the writing, the book layout, their feelings, knowledge learned, and even typos with page numbers.

Doesn't it make you shake your head when you see an established book on the market with reviews dated from a couple of years ago, complaining about typos and layout mistakes which are still present 5 years later? It tells us that some publishers or authors do not read reviews. But more often, it says they do not care enough about little pieces of advice that can be used to improve a book's layout, resulting in an updated edition.

Once publishers and authors really start to take all reviews seriously, to see their books as works in progress, and to take appropriate action, they significantly increase their quality of books, sales, and satisfaction rates. Too often we just move on to a more promising project or a new interest, before taking the time to improve what we already have.

To further illustrate the importance of reviews, as well as their critical feedback mechanism, I want to invite you to visit the Amazon page[56] of young adult author Amanda Hocking, who was one of the early self-publishing Kindle stars.[57] When you browse her books, you will notice that some of them have over 900 reviews, while others have 0 or just a handful of reviews. How is it possible that a successful author with millions of copies sold has such a huge spread between the books?

---

[56] https://www.amazon.com/kindle-dbs/entity/author/B003H4L762

[57] https://www.theguardian.com/books/2012/jan/12/amanda-hocking-self-publishing

One obvious answer is that Amanda has different formats in her list (such as a hardcover version or a CD), as well as some "orphan files" with weird titles or very high prices. But what you also see by taking a closer look is that some books reach "critical mass" and others don't. The ones who don't simply die. And not surprisingly, out of the ones with less than 10 reviews, ratings are low as well. When analyzing such statistics mathematically, you see that there are clear correlations and data points supporting the three review rules stated at the beginning of this chapter.

Basic rules for book reviews

1) No reviews = No sales

2) The more reviews -> The more sales

3) The more positive reviews -> The higher the conversion rates, and the other way around

So what's paramount is to give reviews the importance in book marketing that they really have. They truly make or break books.

To finish this chapter, I want to share with you the results of private research I did with my team. We analyzed the qualitative content of "top reviews" of

100 books on Amazon (51 fiction books, 49 non-fiction advice books)[58] in order to test assumptions and to get a deeper understanding of characteristics readers care and communicate about.

What we found out, by analyzing almost 600 reviews for these books, was that - supporting our core assumption - there is a big difference in what is important in fiction and what's important in advice books. Also, factors that often do not get taken so seriously, such as layout (formatting, typos) or language (easy to read, clear language), get referenced often.

As you can see by looking at the results, in non-fiction books "value" is a primary factor, mentioned in 74% of all reviews. What was interesting to observe for me was that in 14% of all NF reviews, layout was an important factor, although many books were not outstanding in this field. In most cases where the layout was really good (including checklists, nice typography, illustrations, etc.) this was also mentioned in the reviews. This shows that layout is indeed

---

[58] Private Research conducted on Amazon.com in October 2019

important and has the power to be a convincing factor if done properly.

In fiction books, the factors "storytelling" and "language" are critical and mentioned in even more than 90% of analyzed reviews. The paramount take-away is to focus on these characteristics in order to improve ratings and reader satisfaction.

Number of books analyzed - 100 (NF- 49 , F- 51)
Number of reviews analyzed - 581 (NF- 299 , F -282)

NF (299 reviews)
Storytelling mentioned in only **6.5%** of the reviews
Providing Value mentioned in **74%** of the reviews
Layout mentioned in **14%** of the reviews
Language mentioned in **17%** of the reviews

F (282 reviews)
Storytelling mentioned in **72%** of the reviews
Providing Value mentioned in **10%** of the reviews
Layout mentioned in **5%** of the reviews
Language mentioned in **33 %** of the reviews

I want to finish Secret #6 by sharing my favorite quote about reviews, which is:

"Reviews are the lifeblood of books in the digital age."

"Reviews are the lifeblood of books in the digital age."[59] They not only have critical economic importance but also provide much needed feedback to learn and to improve books.

So my advice is to not only focus on having lots of positive reviews, but also to analyze the content carefully, in order to grow your sales and to make you a better writer, author, and publisher.

---

[59] Personal quote, October 2019

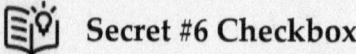

📖 Secret #6 Checkbox

📝 Core Insights:

✓ Reviews are the lifeblood of books in the digital age

✓ 95% of online shoppers read online reviews before purchasing products online [according to 2017 study]

✓ Providing value is the most critical satisfaction factor mentioned for non-fiction reviews, whereas storytelling is in fiction

✓ Remember the basic rules for book reviews [No reviews = No sales, The more reviews -> The more sales

✓ The more positive reviews -> The higher the conversion rates, and the other way around

🔧 Exercises

1) What is your strategy for getting reviews right now?

2) Do you already use a tactic similar to the "surprise gift strategy"?

3) What can you learn from the qualitative message of the reviews you already have?

7

🐦 The Early Bird Catches The Worm

*I*n 2007, I went for an exchange semester to the US, to Oregon State University. It's still one of the best memories I have from my time as a student. The campus was huge, modern, and overall student life on campus was fantastic. I also met a lot of international students and established connections for life.

After having been asked a couple of times to connect with them on Facebook, which I had never heard of, I decided it was time to check out what Facebook actually was.

I went online and registered for the site to connect with students I met. I was hooked quickly and I realized that this social network was onto something. I also realized that creating a Facebook page was easy, and that pages could grow really quickly from just a few members to thousands or even tens of thousands of fans.

Eventually, I started to work in a social media agency which was fully focused on Facebook. We had a great time designing and implementing social media campaigns for corporate clients. Growth rates were fantastic.

At that time, I was not sure about the main take-away from this episode. But years later, when I was already in business with Scribando | Novelify, it became very clear to me that the core insight was how powerful it was to latch on to a trend early. The rewards for early entrants catching a big wave in business are so much higher than the rewards for the players catching the second wave. Very often, it is also not possible to really profit from trends if you are too late. You need to be early.

We have seen the importance of being early[60] and catching a trend numerous times in business, such as

---

[60] The emphasis is on being early and not first. Google, Facebook, and Amazon have certainly not been the first companies in their fields, but their growth was still fueled by catching the immense wave of a trend being created.

with Google, which was not the first search engine of course, but still within the first wave of major players fulfilling the growing need of a great search experience; with Zynga[61], one of the early social game developers on Facebook, the creator behind viral games such as Farmville, reaching 10 million daily active users (DAU) within just six weeks; or with "Toniebox"[62], a more recent example of a German company, whose "listening boxes for kids" have grown into a household name in German-speaking countries within just two years.

And the importance of being early is not any different with books. Especially when we focus on book marketing. The big publishing houses had to learn their lesson painfully regarding e-commerce, when they had to sit still and observe Amazon taking over the online retail space for books, as well as consuming a huge portion of self-publishing with its Kindle Direct Publishing service.

And authors realized quickly around 10 years ago that self-publishing was more than a short-lived trend, but instead a bigger shift that would alter the playing field

---

[61] Source: Wikipedia: https://en.wikipedia.org/wiki/Zynga
[62] https://tonies.de/

forever. Today Amazon's KDP service is the absolute market leader in self-publishing, with sources referencing its book market share in self-published books as up to 85% [63]. Amazon definitely caught the wave early and grew tremendously. Early self-publishing stars like Amanda Hocking[64] in the U.S.A. or B.C. Schiller in Germany have profited immensely from being early.

However, I would not draw a complete picture by only talking about areas related to book marketing, such as distribution and availability. Trends are relevant for the core field book publishing a lot as well, such as with formats (eg. ebooks, audiobooks), publishing processes (eg. lean book publishing), as well as book genres (eg. growth and decline of genres).

A fantastic example was provided by J.K. Rowling with Harry Potter. When she published the first novel, *Harry Potter and the Philosopher's Stone*, in 1997, nobody wanted to touch fantasy stories, as Michelle Smith,

---

[63] Source: Kindlepreneur: https://kindlepreneur.com/best-self-publishing-companies/

[64] Source. Learn more https://www.theguardian.com/books/2012/jan/12/amanda-hocking-self-publishing

senior lecturer in literature at Deakin University [65], told ABC. Fantasy stories were seen as old-fashioned. But Rowling created something new. She added wizards, witches, and magic, bringing new life to the formula. Belle Alderman, the director of the National Centre for Australian Children's Literature at the University of Canberra, even said "the series was the first to blur the line between children's and adult's books."[66]

Rowling's success could be more related to catching a trend early than we had assumed so far. We can also learn that there are frequent opportunities in classical aspects of book publishing, such as new or changing book genres, hot and trending book topics (eg. the latest cooking trend, a new celebrity, a hotly debated phenomenon, etc.) and trending formats (such as short stories, audiobooks, podcasts and conversational stories), to catch and to benefit from.

However, talking about the benefits of being early is one thing. What's even more important, from my experience working personally with more than 100

---

[65] Source: https://www.abc.net.au/news/2017-06-26/harry-potter-effect-how-seven-books-changed-childrens-publishing/8630254
[66] Source: https://www.abc.net.au/news/2017-06-26/harry-potter-effect-how-seven-books-changed-childrens-publishing/8630254

authors and publishers from around the world, is to talk about the costs of being late and of trying to be successful in a market where you have little experience.

A good observation can be made by looking at job postings related to "book launches," "ghostwriting," and "book marketing support" on freelancer webpages, such as Upwork. Many postings unveil author and publisher intentions to follow outdated tactics, combined with inexperience about book marketing. You can read about requirements and expectations, such as "launching book to 100K copies sold," "social media management for aspiring influencer," "getting Amazon bestseller badge quickly," or "ghostwriting Keto Diet book" (which is probably book number 10,000 on that topic already on the market).

Being active on portals like Upwork as a professional[67] can get a little crazy sometimes, but of course I am not here to throw blame. Upwork is a place for connecting with professionals who can help, so that is all fine. What I want to make you aware of, though, is that unfortunately lots of these postings find an agency or

---

[67] Here is my Upwork profile:
https://www.upwork.com/freelancers/~01a883a70099dc1746

a freelancer who will fulfill the client's need without much questioning or a specific background in book marketing, resulting in actions and campaigns that are simply far from being effective in the current landscape.

And honestly, my heart is bleeding every time I see great book projects petering out because of outdated marketing tactics.

Here you have the author who invested a year writing his book, months into polishing, editing, and formatting it with professional help, often investing thousands of dollars, who is finally able to publish it on the market, only to realize that the current approach is not good enough. For me, personally, it is painful. It's one of the factors that keep me most motivated about what I do on a daily basis, as I want to keep as many authors as possible from this painful cycle.

It definitely is one of the aspects I am most passionate about regarding my job, namely, to help my clients with the latest strategies for success, and to save them from going on overcrowded paths that, most of the time, lead to nowhere.

The good thing is that I see a development in the market. Both publishers and authors see more and more that it is beneficial to catch marketing trends early. Clear indicators are the commercial success of self-publisher support companies, like Self Publishing School[68], Kindlepreneur, or KDSPY, as well as outcomes, such as sales figures of self-publishers, and the strong performance of established publishers in the audiobook sector over the last couple of years.

I've even developed my own contribution to helping support authors and publishers in caching book marketing waves early, with my company Scribando (www.scribando.com). In case you haven't, I highly recommend that you sign up for the service and give it a try. My goal is that this service becomes the best investment for a publisher in terms of staying up-to-date on the best book marketing opportunities in the market.

So what should you be doing as an author right now[69], in order to catch the worm? What are the main marketing trends?

---

[68] Source: Self Publishing School: https://self-publishingschool.com/

[69] Time of writing: December, 2019

My answer at the time of writing (late 2019) is straightforward: right now you should be on the forefront of "audio first," "automated book sales funnels," and "AI related to content production." Audio is already happening, as you can see by the growth rates of audiobooks and the success of Audible in recent years. But there is still big potential for audiobooks related to ebooks (just do a search for a keyword on Amazon vs. Audible, to compare the numbers of audiobooks and ebooks on the market).

The most important aspect, though, is to think "audio first." This means you should at first think about questions like, "How would that sound?" "Is that a topic for audio?" etc... Ideally, start with producing an audiobook first.

The next area is Amazon's Alexa. Amazon says it sold over 100 million Alexa-powered gadgets before the beginning of 2019[70], and the catalogue of skills has grown from just 130 upon its release in 2016 to over

---

[70] Source: CNBC https://www.cnbc.com/2019/09/28/amazon-alexa-growth-has-investors-questioning-the-business-model.html

100,000 skills as of September 2019.[71] Once you have an audiobook, creating an Alexa skill in order to promote your book or creating added value for your audiobook is the next step. Today, almost no one is doing that, but my data and insight suggests that this will change quickly and provide a big opportunity in the upcoming years.

The next major area to be in early is AI related to content production. There are already numerous applications and companies offering services in the following three areas, all substantial for authors.

1) Content production: Speech to Text (related to speed) makes producing a book much faster

2) Content production (content automation): Content automation supported by AI. You start a text, AI continues to write a story

3) Book editing (with AI): You provide the raw manuscript, software makes a book out of it

---

[71] Source: Statista:
https://www.statista.com/statistics/912856/amazon-alexa-skills-growth/

It will take some time for commercial readiness in these applications. But once that readiness for marketing has been reached, the wave will grow quickly, and you should not miss it.

I want to finish this chapter with my perspective on the popular quote: "The early bird catches the worm but the second mouse gets the cheese"[72] by advising: "Be both."

> "Be both the early bird that catches the worm and the second mouse that gets the cheese."

The most successful authors and publishers I work with have a great attitude toward staying on top of the latest market developments and opportunities. But they are also wise enough to wait for proven concepts and tools to develop around an opportunity. You do not have to have the expenses of the first mover. That's why, at Scribando, we have also decided to test opportunities whenever possible ourselves, before communicating the insights with our members.

---

[72] Source unknown:
https://quoteinvestigator.com/2013/01/25/second-mouse/

The next secret will teach you how not only how to be the early bird, but more importantly how to be the second mouse which gets the cheese. So read on and discover a proven concept for reverse-engineering successful book publishing models and businesses.

 Secret #7 Checkbox

 Core Insights:

✓ Publishers and authors who catch trends early can exploit advantages and quick growth

✓ It is not about being first, it is about being early and being the second mouse that gets the cheese

⌗ Exercises

1) Are you using services or processes in order to stay up to date on the latest book marketing developments and opportunities? If not, establish a process.

2) What are great opportunities you are aware of that you could tap right now?

8

💲 Follow The Money [And Reverse Engineering Books]

What do the fields of mechanical engineering, military or commercial espionage, e-commerce, and software engineering have in common with book publishing?

You have no clue? Gotcha! I totally understand. Hopefully I've got your attention, because I'm about to tell you. Secret #8 is worth gold to everyone who applies this secret to their book publishing businesses.

What these fields have in common is that they all benefit from the application of reverse engineering. Reverse engineering is the process of developing detailed design information from an existing part or product and an understanding of how it works.[73]

Reverse engineering is about finding something that works, analyzing and understanding it and, in a consequent step (technically distinct from reverse engineering)[74], using the knowledge gained for improving and modeling your own processes. And this is exactly what many successful authors and publishers have done for years, in order to be commercially successful and to beat their competition. I recommend you to do the same. And you should do that by starting to "follow the money" as a first step.

So how do you start with "following the money"? The quickest way to do that is by opening bestseller lists and analyzing sales rankings of books at major retailers, such as Amazon. Go through the first 10 books of major lists, and analyze their book marketing keys. Figure out what they do to be successful. Check out their webpages and observe how they present themselves and their books. Once you take a deep

---

[73] Source: NPD Solutions: https://www.npd-solutions.com/remethodology.html

[74] Source: Wikipedia: https://en.wikipedia.org/wiki/Reverse_engineering

look at the most successful players and start learning from them, you realize more quickly the gap that stands between you and them.

Once you see the gap, you can start to close it by modelling and adapting what successful market players do. Success often speaks for itself. It is hard to hide.

"Success often speaks for itself. It is hard to hide."

So modelling successful authors and publishers is one important aspect of Secret #8. True mastery cannot be achieved, though, if you are not clear on what you want to achieve in the first place. Goal clarity will help you to look for exact role models, as well as envisioning the kind of books and marketing tactics that you need to create in order to reach those publishing goals.

I have recently created a Slideshare presentation on that topic, "How to reach your author goals by reverse engineering your dream book."[75] I recommend you take a look at it.

Source: Reverse Engineering your dream book, © Albert Griesmayr, 2019 https://www.slideshare.net/griesmayr/how-to-reach-your-author-goals-by-reverse-engineering-your-dream-book

In the following, I invite you to do an exercise with me, based on the presentation. It's an exercise that you can apply either to a book project you have planned or a book project you are marketing right now.

---

[75] You can find the presentation by following this link: https://www.slideshare.net/griesmayr/how-to-reach-your-author-goals-by-reverse-engineering-your-dream-book

---

⌖ Follow The Money Exercise

1) Get clarity on your publisher goals (Full-time author? Amount of copies sold, visibility, or sales?)

2) Modeling and defining the needed outcome (Go through the 7 book marketing keys)

3) Create the action step to reach goals (Make a plan to get the results)

The exercise is all about finding the best way to reach your author goals, with the help of modeled players who have already achieved your goals. Defining your goals is quite straightforward (1); what's more difficult is to model and define the needed outcome and the key elements as closely as possible (2). To make things more concrete, I am sharing with you a personal story and my concrete example for the "Follow the money" exercise.

The person that I am modeling is Russell Brunson, founder of Clickfunnels, who has sold at least 250,000 copies of his books *Expert Secrets* and *DotCom Secrets* (April, 2018) [76] through Amazon, his publisher, and his

---

[76] Source: Marketing Secrets Blog, Russell Brunson, 2018: https://marketingsecrets.com/sell-book-amazon-sales-funnel/

own book funnels. I am a big fan of Russell, as he is a true marketing genius and keeps inspiring the digital marketing industry not only with his wisdom, but also with his concrete applications of sales funnels, which he and others have applied very successfully to books as well. So my choice is quite obvious and a well-suited example, as he has already reached the exact goals I want to reach with methods that align with me as well.

So here is my exercise based on an analysis of Russell's books and business.

ⵑ Follow The Money Exercise [Modeling Russell Brunson, Founder ClickFunnels]

1) <u>My goals:</u>

  - more visibility and sales
  - book sales automation important
  - testing webpage based book sales funnels
  - promoting Scribando.com
  - adding credibility
  - having more time for consulting by sharing already formulated insights with clients

2) <u>Needed outcome:</u> [primarily based on Russell as an example]

> - Need to have strong manuscript and 7 book marketing keys
> - Particular focus on the funnel on my page and Scribando.com
> - Funnel needs to have upsell products, so that I can invest in paid advertising
> - Podcast or video series on the 10 secrets
>
> 3) Action steps:
>
> - Going the extra mile for creating a great book
> - Building funnel on my webpage and integrating upsells
> - Once the book is out, create YouTube- and Facebook video series on the 10 secrets
> - Get help for paid advertising campaign on FB and YT

I invite you to visit some of Russell's websites, such as "Expert Secrets,"[77] "Clickfunnels,"[78] or his marketing blog "Marketing Secrets,"[79] so that you get a better understanding for my analysis. Examining and studying a process that brings you the results that

---

[77] https://expertsecrets.com/freebook

[78] https://www.clickfunnels.com/

[79] https://marketingsecrets.com/

you want to achieve online is priceless. The internet has made reverse-engineering so much easier. It opens up true shortcuts that will free your time for what truly matters most to you.

Here are some important notes for your personal "follow-the-money" process. These will help you to avoid common pitfalls. Make sure that you:

– Do not get blinded by something that looks good or brings results indiscriminately; pick a role-model that has achieved what you want to achieve (be specific)

– Analyze potential success elements with care (sometimes there are tiny things that make a huge difference)

– Simplify whatever you can. It's difficult to start with the most advanced system. Break it down and start with something very simple, based on your role model

– Understand the underlying principles, formulas, and mechanics behind processes in order to learn correctly

Now, it's your turn to do the exercise. Find at least one publishing role model who has achieved what you are striving for and who you want to learn from. Analyze what they are doing and create your own action steps to get the results you are looking for.

Applying Secret #8 will put your publishing business and author career on steroids, as you will be able to reach your goals much faster by following proven recipes and formulas.

 Secret #8 Checkbox

 Core Insights:

✓ Follow the money and look for authors and publishers who have reached what you want to accomplish

✓ Reverse-engineer their books and systems and get an understanding of why they are successful

Exercises

1) Do the "follow the money" exercise and reverse engineer one of your role models

---

9

☺ Post Sales Magic

I want to start this chapter with a question. What do you think: How much more expensive is it to acquire a new customer versus retaining an existing one?

a) 2-3 times

b) 5-10 times or

c) 5-25 times

According to numerous studies, acquiring a new customer is anywhere from 5 to 25 times more expensive than retaining an existing one[80]. So if you guessed c) you chose the correct answer.

---

[80] Source: Harvard Business Review, 2014

https://hbr.org/2014/10/the-value-of-keeping-the-right-customers

"Acquiring a new customer is anywhere from five to 25 times more expensive than retaining an existing one.[81]"

And still, we as marketers behave in quite an unorthodox way. Most of us (including myself) have the natural tendency to focus on acquiring new customers and making new sales, instead of nurturing existing ones and focusing deeply on the customer journey of existing clients. Based on studies, our behavior is simply a mistake, a trick that our mind is playing on us. This chapter is aimed at convincing you that it pays off disproportionately. We need to break this wrong mindset and to focus on "post sales phases" instead. I invite you to follow me on a journey, an adventure to "Post Sales Magic Land" [PSML].

"Post Sales Magic Land" is a place that is filled with happy clients. They have crossed the border by paying their entry fee and realized after entering that they not only got what was promised, but even more than that. Their expectations have not only been fulfilled, they have been excelled. And now as clients are feeling happy, they are starting to make the new land their own. They start exploring for further

---

[81] Source: Source: Harvard Business Review, 2014
https://hbr.org/2014/10/the-value-of-keeping-the-right-customers

opportunities. They prepare themselves for a long stay. They start shopping around and spreading the word about their great experience by calling their friends. And as long as they are not disappointed, they will stay happy customers of Post Sales Magic Land.

Wouldn't it be great to be the mayor of PSML? I bet it would. PSML is full of "post sales magic." Let's explore further.

Post Sales Magic is about making a fundamental shift: a shift in thinking. The shift away from the focus on "making the sale" to "starting with the sale." It is all about acknowledging that making a book sale is just a start or a stopover in the relationship with the reader, always embedded in a bigger process. It's about realizing that our job as authors and publishers has not been completed when we have sold a book; it has just started, instead.

In this chapter, you'll not only learn why focusing on the post-sale phase is so beneficial. Even more importantly, you'll learn how to create reader experiences that celebrate "post sales magic" in a way that not only makes your readers happy, but which is also financially profitable. So stay with me.

Let's explore the question of why investing in an amazing post-sales phase is so beneficial. We already talked about the high costs of acquiring new customers vs. selling more to existing ones, but there is way more than that.

In fact, by focusing on the post-sales phase, you are able to create happy customers who, in turn, will help you to sell more books and grow your business. Think about yourself! What do you do when you find a product that not only fulfilled your expectations, but even over-delivered? You will likely use the product, share it with others, maybe give feedback or provide a review, and want to buy more of the same brand. You will not complain to customer service, cause negative experiences with company reps, or make the product designers unhappy.

A happy customer (in our case a happy reader) will bring you the results you are striving for. Focusing on the customer experience and designing an amazing "post sales experience" is one of the best things that you can do as a publisher or author.

I now invite you to take a look at the following checklist, which shows you 15 proven tactics to create "post sales magic" for your readers. Most of these tactics below are used by my clients and other publishers with success.

Post Sales Magic Tactics [15 Proven PSM Tactics To Improve Reader Satisfaction And Increase Book Sales]

- Create the best book you can (apply secrets 1,2,3,..)
- Work with a fantastic surprise gift
- Add bonus value on your webpage
- Put a "feedback request box" into your book
- Offer useful upsell products
- Create email automation that adds value
- Invest in creating a launch team
- Work with book publishing professionals (eg. editors, formatters, translators, marketers..)
- Apply lean book publishing principles (such as testing your book before launching big)
- Write a book series
- Promote other books from you at the end of your book
- Have upsell products in place

- Read your book reviews and fix what can be fixed (publish revised editions)

- Trigger built-in virality (eg. include partner exercises, surprising book elements, etc.)

- Add unadvertised bonuses that readers did not expect (eg. thank you gift, book summaries, audiobook free, etc.)

Once you have achieved a high level of customer satisfaction, it gets far easier to earn more by offering related or upsell products. Take a look at the following list of possible related and upsell products that you can use to earn more from the readers and clients that you already have.

List of possible related and upsell products

- other book formats (eg. audiobook, paperback, etc.)

- other books in a series

- online courses

- paid webinars

- online or real-world workshops

- affiliate products
- related books and products
- online programs
- member areas

Post sales magic creates true win-win situations. Readers win because they get product experiences they truly love. And publishers win because they receive positive feedback, reviews, and more sales down the line.

In order to make things easy, I boiled Secret #9 down to a simple formula: the post sales magic formula. Apply the formula and be rewarded.

Post Sales Magic Formula

Create a fantastic reader experience that not only fulfills but excels reader expectations and provides plenty of opportunities to stay in touch and to purchase more from you.

One of the most important questions that you should ask yourself is: "What should my readers do after they have purchased and read my book?" Take a break for a second, get a pen and paper, and do the following exercise:

Exercise: Post-Sales Reader Behavior: *"What are"* vs. *"What should* my readers be doing after having read my book?"

Get pen and paper and answer the following questions about your readers post-sales experience. Then write down a concrete action step that you can implement for getting desired results.

1) Do your readers think that they have read a fantastic/valuable book?

2) Do they tell a friend about it?

3) Do they post on social media?

4) Do they visit your webpage and leave their contact information?

5) Do they purchase a different book from you?

Once you have done the exercise, you will have concrete action steps for getting closer to creating "post sales magic." Act on them and increase reader satisfaction bit by bit.

I want to finish Chapter 9 with a quote by management professor Michael LeBoeuf [82]:

"A satisfied customer is the best business strategy of all."
-Michael LeBoeuf

A satisfied customer *is* the best business strategy of all. It should come as no surprise when I tell you that without satisfied, loyal customers, you will never have a successful business. [83]

I couldn't agree more with Michael LeBoeuf, and this is certainly true for books as well. Do not fall for the mistake a lot of authors make of focusing on the sale and missing the big opportunity of "post sales magic." Act like a skilled book marketer instead. Understand that your job and the real opportunity for book wealth has just started with a book sale.

Change your focus towards reader satisfaction and stop seeing the book sale as the end point. Always see

---

[82] Source: Wikipedia:
https://en.wikipedia.org/wiki/Michael_LeBoeuf

[83] Source: By Michael LeBoeuf:
https://therestaurantboss.com/leboeuf-satisfied-customer/ (exact source of original publication unknown)

it as a starting point or interstation before receiving feedback, getting a reader on your email-list, making another book sale, selling an upsell product or spreading word of mouth. Change your mindset and increase your odds of success substantially.

📖 **Secret #9 Checkbox**
📝 Core Insights:
✓ Post Sales Magic is about focusing on reader satisfaction and realizing that the book sale is just the start ✓ Use the "Post Sales Magic Formula" [Create a fantastic reader experience that not only fulfills but excels reader expectations and provides plenty of opportunities to stay in touch and to purchase more from you.]
⫲ Exercises
1) Analyze how you can apply the post sales magic formula to your books. 2) Do the post-sales-reader behavior exercise and list action steps to increase your PSM

10

⚙ The Holy Grail: Book Sales Automation

ook Marketing Secret #10 is the holy grail of book marketing. It is the ultimate ideal outcome of all author and publisher efforts and the result of mastery of all previous book marketing secrets. It also shows a core element of the beauty of book publishing. It is the chance for creating a stream of passive income.

A stream of passive income created from an "automated book sales system" that lives and breathes on its own, a stream that makes your book publishing venture profitable. That means I am not talking about selling 50 copies, for instance, that bring $4 USD royalties/book a month, resulting in a revenue of $200 USD.

No. What I am talking about is the type of passive income that stays in your pocket at the end of the month. Profit. Revenue/royalties from book sales, minus advertising and other costs, resulting in pure profit from your book ventures. That's the kind of income that has made selected publishers and top authors truly wealthy over the last decades. Due to increased competition, achieving market success has certainly become more difficult over the last 10 years. But passive income from books is still a very achievable goal and a reality for many authors, publishers, and publishing businesses in the market.

I just recently talked again to owners of a Kindle publishing business, who were able to scale up their business from 0 to more than 300 books (which they fully control), bringing in a revenue of more than $25,000 USD per month, all built in less than 2 years. Pretty amazing. Is their business profitable? Yes, it is.

These founders are ambitious and they have far bigger goals. That's why they invest heavily in new titles, education, and advertising. So they might not generate a big profit at the end of a month yet; but if they stopped investing and publishing today, they would already have built a very solid passive income business, all made from books.

To fully understand different ways of how book sales automation can work, you need to understand your "book sales system" first.

Below, find my visualization of the "automated book sales system" for this book, *Book Marketing Secrets*. It is based on the 3-step model "Attraction - Conversion – Retention."[84] Attraction involves steps to attract customers. Conversion refers to the process of making them a customer, requiring that they are in touch with your sales page. And retention is all about keeping and growing revenue from existing customers. The model is simple, beautiful, and effective. You can also draw it out quickly (once you have the data) and make your "automated book sales system" understandable quite easily. As I created the model before I launched, the cited numbers, such as the cost for acquiring a reader and the expected conversion rates, are my estimates and plan to launch with. I am planning on updating the numbers in a revised future edition. Let's take a look at my model below:

---

[84] Source: Albert Griesmayr, 2019

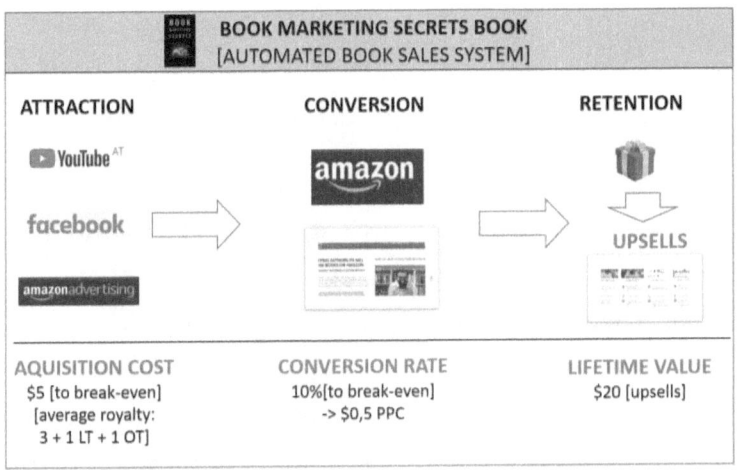

"Automated book sales system" - Book: Book Marketing Secrets"
© Albert Griesmayr, 2019

Traffic should primarily come from:

- YouTube video series + paid YT advertising

- Facebook video series + paid FB advertising

- Amazon ads + Amazon organic search

Conversion [rates & sales pages]:

- There is one sales page on Amazon and one sales page on my website

- I am willing to spend up to $5 for each new reader who purchases the book (to break even)

<u>Retention [upsell products]:</u>

- Readers should sign up on my webpage (50% of my readers), because of my thank you gift
- As long as they are on my list, I can make them aware of my other (upsell) products, such as my online program, the Scribando service, and other books

So in a nutshell, that's my plan and visualization of my book marketing system. I will launch the book to 10K readers [Book Marketing Secret #5], and have the goal of getting 200 new readers at break even [$1,000 revenue] at $1,000 expense. To make this calculation work, I calculate with $5 in revenue ($3 revenue + $1 lifetime value + $1 organic sales increase), as below that point paid advertising gets increasingly difficult, even for a very targeted product.

On the other hand, when looking at the lifetime value of my audience, I estimate a new reader to be worth much more than $5, so I am totally fine with my calculation of spending $5 for each new reader, without any loss and with acquiring new readers basically for free. When you combine that with the fact that you can scale up such a system, it quickly gets very powerful for authors and publishers who are able to make such a system work.

You can also see that this book is not a passive income machine for me. My main goal is to share my knowledge at an affordable price (because that's my passion) and most importantly to acquire new customers basically for free. These will hopefully, ultimately, spend more later, as my business is 100% focused on making them more successful with their books. I truly hope that you will be one of those customers that I can convince to stay longer and do more business with me along the line.

So, summed up, *Book Marketing Secrets* is primarily a marketing tool for me. But let's go back to you and your "automated book sales system." I invite you to get pen and paper and to draw your own current (or intended) version of your book sales system.

🖧 Draw Your Own Book Sales System | Exercise
Take pen and paper and draw your own book sales system with the help of "Attraction, Conversion, Retention" and the visual example of the "BMS book sales system" displayed in this book.

Start with the channels your readers are coming from, and put concrete numbers if you have them (if not, your homework is to get those numbers).

Afterwards, look at your point of sale(s). What can be done there to improve your conversion rates? And as a final step, look at your retention. What are you doing to keep in touch with your readers (eg. email signup), to keep them engaged (eg. built-in virality elements), to drive them to your other products (eg. other books)? Make a list of things to improve in this area.

The ideal scenario is that you are able to optimize your system to a level where it keeps itself running. A system in which you put $1 USD in, and $2 USD emerges at the end of the day. Ideally, a system that is scalable with paid advertising. Once you have achieved this level, you have achieved true mastery. With mastery, you can bring it to a level where you can live on your books and writing, the dream of every writer, but which so few of us achieve in the end.

I hope that my calculation also reminded you once more why it is so important to have upsell products. If you have only one book on the market and you generate a royalty of around three or four dollars, then it gets almost impossible to achieve positive return on advertising spent with the book alone. That's why most successful authors and publishers have lines of products such as book series, and related products on top of that. Your tolerable cost of acquisition of a new customer changes dramatically with just one more product down the line. Imagine you are selling an online course for the price of $37 on top of your non-fiction book. Suddenly you are able to spend up to $10 for a new client. Without the upsell product, you can spend only $3.

And don't forget that you do not always need to create your own products. You can also act as an affiliate and earn commissions for products that are already on the market. Summed up, your calculations change dramatically with upsell products and also decide if you are able to compete in the market with paid advertising at all. I highly recommend that you dive deep into your own book sales system. Invest time and resources to make that work and to achieve the point of mastery, which frees you to spend more time on writing and creating and all the things you truly love.

Never forget Book Marketing Secret #10. Strive for it, make it one of your ultimate goals, in order to achieve true book marketing mastery.

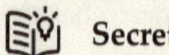 Secret #10 Checkbox

Core Insights:

✓ Books are fantastic products for getting passive income

✓ Every author/publishers should have an understanding of their automated "book sales funnel" which covers Attraction, Conversion, and Retention

Exercises

Take pen and paper.

1) Draw your "book sales funnel." Include numbers whenever possible.

2) If you advertise, do you have a positive ROAS?

3) What steps can you take to improve your level of book sales automation?

Cheatsheet

BOOK MARKETING SECRETS CHEATSHEET
DISCOVER ALL SECRETS AT A GLANCE | PERFECT FOR PINBOARDS

 SECRET 01 THE BOOK IS THE STAR
-> CREATE THE BEST BOOK YOU CAN

 SECRET 02 THE 7 BOOK MARKETING KEYS
-> COVER, TITLE, DESCRIPTION, LAYOUT
AUTHOR/PUBLISHER, REVIEWS, MARKETING STRATEGY

SECRET 03 THE 80/20 RULE OF BOOK MARKETING
-> 20% EFFORT / 80% OUTCOME | 80% IMPORTANCE BOOK KEYS

 **SECRET 04**
LEAN BOOK PUBLISHING
-> PUBLISH LEAN - GET FEEDBACK

SECRET 05
10K READER LAUNCH
-> 10K -> 1K -> 1H-

SECRET 06 REVIEWS
-> GET AS MUCH AS YOU CAN

SECRET 07 EARLY BIRD
-> CATCH TRENDS EARLY

SECRET 08 MONEY
-> FOLLOW & REVERSE ENGINEER

SECRET 09 POST SALES
-> MAKE READERS HAPPY

SECRET 10 AUTOMATE YOUR BOOK MARKETING
-> UNDERSTAND READER FLOWS AND AUTOMATE YOUR PROCESSES

www.albertgriesmayr.com

Final Words

Dear author,

First of all, I want to thank you for taking the time to read this book. It means a lot to me, as the core of my business career is to help authors like you to create successful book projects and publishing careers.

If there is one thing that I would love you to take away from this book, it's an improved mindset toward the critical success factors described in the secrets, such as having a relentless focus on producing great book, performing data-driven marketing, and applying a lean publishing approach.

If you have the 10 secrets in mind consistently then I am very confident that having bought and read this book will bring a positive ROI for your books and career as well.

I truly hope that this book was of high value to you. I hope that you have learned skills which will help you to better market your book. If you have not yet taken a look at Scribando (www.scribando.com), I highly recommend that you do so, as my service will help you to not only stay up-to-date on what is happening in the market, but also be informed about the latest success strategies on how to sell books.

In the end, to win big as an author, you need to master both timeless book marketing knowledge and the latest success strategies. With this book and Scribando, you have the perfect knowledge setup for selling lots of books.

I also want to invite you to check out the surprise gift that I have prepared for you. It will also help you to grow your author career. In addition, when you sign up at my webpage, you can stay in touch with me and won't miss new releases and book marketing insights.

Claim Your Surprise Gift

Thank you so much for purchasing my book. To thank you, I've prepared a special gift for you that will help you to sell more books. Access it by visiting: www.albertgriesmayr.com/thank-you

As a writer you also know how important it is to get reviews. I always say, "Reviews are the lifeblood of books in the digital age." They can truly make or break books. So I hope that, as a fellow author, you review this book and post your review on Amazon or any other book retailer you purchased the book from. It would mean a lot to me. You can be sure that I read each review. I am happy with each positive one and try to learn from each critique as well.

ASK ME YOUR QUESTIONS
GIVE FEEDBACK AND REVIEW THE BOOK

The most important thing for me in business is to provide value and to leave you, as my reader, satisfied. That's why I invite you to ask me questions and to send me feedback about the book to hello@scribando.com. I will try to get back to you within 24-48 hours. I would love this to be the start of a great relationship between us!

And, of course, I would also love to see an official review posted to Amazon or other book retailers. I read each and every review personally.

I want to close this book by sharing a last quote. It is from the creator of the 100 Day Challenge, Gary Ryan

Blair[85], who says, "Finishing strong is the only respectable way to finish."

> "Finishing strong is the only respectable way to finish."
> *Gary Ryan Blair*

And I could not agree more with him when it comes to creating successful book projects. Finish strong and make what's already good great. That's an easier way to success than starting all over again.

I wish you all the best in the world, and that you have the success with your books that you dream of.

Best wishes,
Albert Griesmayr
Founder & CEO of Scribando | Novelify
December 1, 2019, Vienna, Austria

---

[85] Source: Gary Ryan Blair: Creator of the 100 Day Challenge
https://www.100daychallenge.com/gary-ryan-blair/

THE END

&

THE BEGINNING OF
YOUR NEXT CHAPTER